T0049797

"For every Christian, nothing compares to the importance of the gospel of Jesus Christ. It is the entry point to new life. Jonny Morrison's *Prodigal Gospel* explores this entry point. He leads us into a deep dive with a deeper gospel and a deeper life with God through Jesus. Theologically faithful, compellingly personal—read this book and walk with Jonny into a deeper gospel."

—**DAVID FITCH**, B. R. Lindner Professor of Evangelical Theology at Northern Seminary and author of *Reckoning with Power*

"In *Prodigal Gospel*, Jonny Morrison presents the good news in high-definition. These pages introduce us to a God who desires to share space with us. Consider this book an invitation to the party that God set up for everyone who's ever wandered."

—**TREY FERGUSON**, author of *Theologizin' Bigger: Homilies on Living Freely and Loving Wholly* and host of the *New Living Treyslation* and *Three Black Men* podcasts

"Too often the gospel becomes a doctrinal formula, rarely good news that we can't wait to live and share. In winsome ways, Jonny Morrison expands our imagination for how Jesus makes a real difference in daily life. And in so doing he expands our vocabulary for ways to share it with a world in need of good news."

—**MANDY SMITH**, pastor and author of *The Vulnerable Pastor and Confessions of an Amateur Saint*

"With humor, storytelling, and compassion, Jonny Morrison offers the gospel back to those whose Christian life has been stripped bare by judgment and fear. *Prodigal Gospel* is a hopeful companion for those looking to renew and reconstruct their faith in a God who is love."

—**MELISSA FLORER-BIXLER**, pastor of Raleigh Mennonite Church and author of *How to Have an Enemy: Righteous Anger and the Work of Peace*

"This book helps us move from a transactional to a relational framework for good news. By using the prodigal parable as the lens to examine things like atonement and sin and the Trinity and heaven, Jonny Morrison helps us shed our legalese, leaving us with a gospel that looks like Jesus. And that is a gift."

—**JEREMY DUNCAN**, founding pastor of Commons Church in Calgary, Alberta, and author of *Upside-Down Apocalypse: Grounding Revelation in the Gospel of Peace*

"In a time when so many are asking big questions about God and what it means to be a part of God's people, Jonny Morrison paints a loving portrait of both. With careful attention to both the text and the cultural layers we bring to our theology, he points us toward a gospel that is truly good news. If you're looking to reorient your faith around toward a vision of hope and belonging, *Prodigal Gospel* is just the companion you need."

—**KATE BOYD**, author of *An Untidy Faith: Journeying Back to the Joy of Following Jesus*, creator of the Threaded Bible studies, and founder of The Remembered Table

Prodigal Gospel

Prodigal Gospel

GETTING LOST and FOUND AGAIN in the GOOD NEWS

Jonny Morrison

Harrisonburg, Virginia

Herald Press
PO Box 866, Harrisonburg, Virginia 22803
www.HeraldPress.com

Library of Congress Cataloging-in-Publication Data
Names: Morrison, Jonny, author.
Title: Prodigal gospel : getting lost and found again in the Good News / Jonny Morrison.
Description: Harrisonburg, Virginia : Herald Press, 2024. | Includes bibliographical
    references.
Identifiers: LCCN 2023058555 (print) | LCCN 2023058556 (ebook) |
    ISBN 9781513813233 (paperback) | ISBN 9781513813240 (hardcover) |
    ISBN 9781513813257 (ebook)
Subjects: LCSH: Prodigal son (Parable) | Christian life—Biblical teaching. | BISAC:
    RELIGION / Christian Ministry / Discipleship | RELIGION / Biblical Studies /
    New Testament / Jesus, the Gospels & Acts
Classification: LCC BT378.P8 M58 2024 (print) | LCC BT378.P8 (ebook) |
    DDC 226.8/06—dc23/eng/20240220
LC record available at https://lccn.loc.gov/2023058555
LC ebook record available at https://lccn.loc.gov/2023058556

Produced in partnership with

Study guides are available for many Herald Press titles at www.HeraldPress.com.

PRODIGAL GOSPEL
© 2024 by Herald Press, Harrisonburg, Virginia 22803. 800-245-7894.
    All rights reserved.
Library of Congress Control Number: 2023058555
International Standard Book Number: 978-1-5138-1323-3 (paperback);
    978-1-5138-1324-0 (hardcover); 978-1-5138-1325-7 (ebook)
Printed in United States of America

All rights reserved. This publication may not be reproduced, stored in a retrieval system, or
transmitted in whole or in part, in any form, by any means, electronic, mechanical, photo-
copying, recording or otherwise without prior permission of the copyright owners.

Unless otherwise noted, scripture text is quoted, with permission, from the COMMON
ENGLISH BIBLE. Copyright © 2011 COMMON ENGLISH BIBLE. All rights reserved.
Used by permission. www.CommonEnglishBible.com. Scripture quotations marked (The
Message) are taken from THE MESSAGE, copyright © 1993, 2002, 2018 by Eugene H.
Peterson. Used by permission of NavPress, represented by Tyndale House Publishers. All
rights reserved. Scripture quotations marked (NIV) are taken from the Holy Bible, New
International Version®, NIV®. Copyright © 1973, 1978, 1984, 2011 by Biblica, Inc.®
Used by permission of Zondervan. All rights reserved worldwide. www.zondervan.com.
The "NIV" and "New International Version" are trademarks registered in the United States
Patent and Trademark Office by Biblica, Inc.® Scripture quotations marked (NRSVue) are
taken from the *New Revised Standard Version* Updated Edition. Copyright © 2021 National
Council of Churches of Christ in the United States of America. Used by permission. All
rights reserved worldwide. Scripture quotations marked (KJV) are taken from the King
James Version.

28 27 26 25 24   10 9 8 7 6 5 4 3 2 1

We're all lost here and we feel right at home.
—**ROBERT FARRAR CAPON**, *Kingdom, Grace, Judgment*[1]

For my fathers

CONTENTS

Foreword

THERE'S A PROBLEM with the world. This much is obvious to nearly everyone. Wars and government corruption, poverty and abuse, a hundred different tragic isms—it doesn't exactly take eyes of faith to see them.

Less obvious is the source of all this trouble. Some believe that the core problem with the world is that people are bad. If so, the primary solution is to persuade them to behave. Religion traditionally offers vital support via an elaborate system of carrots and sticks. Stick: God is watching and threatening flames (or eternal accordion music) for those who misbehave. Carrot: Be good, and God will answer your prayers and give you keys to a sky mansion when you die. The limited effectiveness of the system seems clear from the result. A mansion in the hand, it seems, is worth two in the clouds.

Many would be surprised to learn that the Bible's account is somewhat different. In the Genesis story, the trouble begins not when humans spontaneously go bad but when humans become convinced that God is bad: God is not as generous or reliable as

God claims to be. It is doubt about God's goodness that starts the world's downward spiral—every man, every woman, every snake for themselves, to seize and hold whatever they can.

If Genesis is correct and the world's core wound is a distortion in the image of God, then the solution lies in a different direction than more religious sticks and carrots. What is needed is nothing less than a radical healing in our perception of the character of God. From his teachings and his healings to the game-changing, world-remaking revelation of the cross, this is exactly what Jesus offers.

I have come to believe that the heart of the spiritual journey is a struggle to realign our vision of God with Jesus'—and with Jesus himself. This is not an easy thing to do. After decades as a Christian, even as a Christian leader, I'm only recently becoming aware of all the ways that my life still flows from a shadowed and distorted image. I have often wished for a companion to help me grasp with my soul what I've accepted with my head— that God really is exactly who Jesus says God is.

This is why I was so excited the first time I read *Prodigal Gospel*. In *Prodigal Gospel*, Jonny Morrison has provided the companion for which I've been looking. Jonny explores Jesus' most famous story with theological insight and a keen psychological astuteness that almost had me wondering whether he'd been reading my mail. The book does exactly what all good spiritual guides do—sets the table for transformative spiritual encounter beyond its own pages. It made me hungry to meet with Jesus again, and to believe, really believe, that the story he tells is my own story.

I'm not the only one, I am quite certain, who needs to meet God all over again—I'm not the only one craving good news that is truly good. I pray that you will read this book not just for yourself but also for your neighbors who are longing for a home that they may not even know exists. May you be gripped, body and soul, by the extravagant goodness of God. And may that goodness make you brave and generous and lavish with confetti at every prodigal party—just as Jesus was and still is.

> —Meghan Larissa Good, lead pastor at Trinity Mennonite Church in Phoenix, Arizona, and author of *Divine Gravity: Sparking a Movement to Recover a Better Christian Story*

Introduction

I MET KEV when he started attending this little hipster worship service I curated in 2009—think candles, synth dance parties, and art nights. Kev looked like a real-life anime character—sharp features, dramatic hair (razor bangs, shaved sides, high spikes), with an encyclopedic knowledge of Pokémon. We instantly became friends. Kev had recently become a follower of Jesus and was, and is to this day, a curious and voracious student of faith. He read anything and everything he could about Jesus, theology, and the Bible. We'd sit together for hours, smoking Parliaments, listening to Bright Eyes, and talking about God.

A few years into our friendship I had the joy of baptizing Kev in a mountain lake and shortly after that we, with a few other guys, moved into a house together that my now father-in-law dubbed the Alpha Omega Fraternity House. We'd host Bible studies, cook huge meals for our friends, and talk about Jesus and socialism like we were radicals. After a few years, we all began to move in new directions. I got married and Kev got his own place, but we stayed close.

Over a decade has passed since that time in our lives, but Kev and I still meet to talk about faith, life, and of course, what he's reading. Not long ago, Kev and I were together sharing a pot of tea (how the times have changed us) when our conversation about theology shifted to a conversation about life. That's normal—any real conversation about faith is a conversation about life—but there was something different about this moment. Kev's posture shifted, his voice lowered, and his pace slowed. I'm not always the most emotionally attuned person but I could tell something was on Kev's mind, so I asked him if there was something he wanted to talk about. Kev took a moment and then said, "I don't think God can love me." Kev went on to explain how he feels separated from God, like God is ashamed of him, even despises him. Kev told me how the weight of unlovability had grown since he first became a Christian and how practices like prayer had become fearful encounters with a God who, he believed, was rejecting him. Kev finished by saying the distance and weight felt too heavy and that he'd been seriously contemplating suicide, but he feared suicide would doom him to hell and eternal distance from the God he desperately wanted to belong to.

When I heard the pain in my friend's voice, I began to cry. All I knew to do was hold his hands, look him in the eye and say, "Kev, nothing can separate you from the love of God, not suicide, not anything. I don't want you to take your life and if you choose to, I'll be heartbroken, but I believe with everything that I am that you'll meet Jesus and he'll say, 'It's so good to see you. I'm glad you're home.'" My friend looked at me through his own tears and asked, "You really believe that?" "Yes," I said, "I think that's the gospel."

I really believe that.

YOU DON'T PREACH THE GOSPEL!

We were sitting in my office, late one evening, for a meeting I was absolutely dreading. I knew it was going to be intense—sometimes that happens; you can feel subtext in an email, like a secret code hidden under the pleasantries. I didn't know exactly what we'd be talking about, but I was prepared for it to suck.

Our conversation began nice enough. We caught up and talked about family, vacations, and holiday plans. But eventually, as all things must, the conversation turned to the matter at hand. With heavy sighs and sad expressions, this couple informed me that they had decided to leave our church. I've been a pastor for a while, but I have never adjusted to departures. I want people to arrive and never leave. I know that's selfish, but a boy can dream.

In response, I asked if they would be willing to explain why they were leaving, to provide a little context and background to their decision. They looked at one another, and then towards me with what felt like pity in their eyes, and said, "Because you don't preach the gospel."

To say I was speechless feels dramatic; I'm a trained talky person and am never really without a word, but I can say I was genuinely taken aback. I've been accused of not "preaching the gospel" before, but never by people who had such proximity to me. This couple had heard me teach for years. We had met for coffee, shared meals, and they'd even privileged me with participation in some of the hardest moments of their lives. To say "You don't preach the gospel" felt like a startling affront to our shared history. I wanted to respond by saying, "You know me better than that, you've been with me too long to make an accusation like that." Instead, I asked for more clarity. A subtler protest.

They were ready for my question. This is a thoughtful and articulate couple, and they had not come to this decision lightly. The couple said, "You talk a lot about society, justice, power, and racism, and those are good things, but they aren't the gospel." They continued, "We feel like we're starving for the gospel. We want to hear about our sins and how Jesus' death deals with our sin." Then they finished by saying, "The gospel is about individuals and individual sin, and that is what we need to hear more of."

When they first told me they were leaving, I didn't believe it was because of the gospel. In my mind, we were disagreeing over semantics, language, or secondary issues. Gospel is that one thing we *all* agree on, the very basis of our shared life together and the reason they would talk to me in the first place. But as they articulated their understanding of the gospel, I realized they were right, at least partially. We did disagree, and about more than semantics. We talked for quite a while and eventually met up again to continue our conversation. In our final meeting I remember feeling so profoundly frustrated at how they talked about the gospel that I looked at them, and with a grace I'm not proud of, said, "I vehemently disagree with you." I wish I had chosen my words a little more carefully, because as soon I uttered them, one of them began to cry. But it is true—I do disagree, maybe even vehemently.

FRAGMENTED SPIRITUALITY

I tell you these stories because they illustrate what I believe are two sides of one problem. *Gospel* means *good news*, and for Christians it defines the very center of our faith in Jesus. But something about our good news is amiss when an avid student of theology feels impossibly separated from God. Or when thoughtful Christians cannot and will not see a connection between Jesus and the social problems of our world.

These two stories also represent a broader set of conversations I've had about the gospel over the years. Some were with friends and churchgoers who are frustrated with their experience of the gospel and want more from their faith and church life. And others with Christian leaders who have experienced their fair share of difficult gospel conversations and are now trying to navigate their way forward.

In 2017, researchers at Yale coined the phrase *fragmented spirituality* to describe the kind of frustration many of us are experiencing. Fragmentation is the feeling of a gap—between our faith and world, between the realities of everyday life and the story of God our churches, traditions, and even religious friends are offering. Fragmentation isn't the same as *deconstruction*—the more popular term—but it is similar in that it points to the way questions or experiences can unravel the foundation of faith. Where fragmentation differs is that it emerges from feeling like life is being compartmentalized. Dr. Almeda Wright, the lead researcher in the Yale study, writes, "Regardless of whether youth are enamored with a personal Jesus or actively protesting injustices, there appears to be a chasm between these arenas for them, such that neither informs the other and their spiritual lives remain fragmented or compartmentalized."[1] Something about faith is still meaningful—often the person and words of Jesus—but a chasm has opened between our understanding of faith and our lived experience of it.

I began to experience my own fragmentation in high school. I was raised in a Christian home, and after my father died, my little Christian community became family. As I grew up in the faith, and then began to make it my own, certain questions began to arise about the person we worshiped, Jesus, and the things we said about him. My church talked a lot about wealth and prosperity as a blessing from God, but even as a sixteen-year-old I struggled to understand how our insistence on the blessedness of richness squared with the penniless preacher who said it's very hard for the rich to enter the kingdom of heaven.

When I got a little older, and started engaging with Jesus' Sermon on the Mount, I was confronted with Jesus' teaching to love our enemy. But in my church we had armed security guards who played Secret Service to the lead pastor. One of the greatest challenges came when I began struggling with how Christians could support the American war effort in Iraq. This time, I was at a new church in my first-ever official church leadership role, and as I brought my questions to my friend and pastor, I was told that if I could not support the American military I could not serve on staff.

Moments like these began to unravel something inside of me. They forced me to investigate my faith and interrogate the stories I had inherited. For many, fragmentation began as they watched the repeated murders of men and women of color by police officers. They struggled for an answer, and when they turned to their churches and Christian traditions for hope, they were often met with hostility. For others, unraveling began with the way white evangelicals supported Donald Trump. We could go on, from how faith has been weaponized against the LGBTQI community, to the scapegoating of refugees and immigrants, and to the ways in which faith and the gospel, as it had for my friend Kev, become a heavy and terrifying story of rejection, shame, distance, and hate.

Something is wrong with *our* gospel.

GOOD NEWS ABOUT GOOD NEWS

If you hadn't already guessed, this is a book about the gospel. The gospel is the good news that Jesus has come to reveal something about God and accomplish God's purposes. That's a bit of a vague definition, I know, but the rest of this book is about answering the questions:

1. What does Jesus reveal?

2. What does Jesus accomplish?

And I hope that by answering these two questions, we can answer the most important question of all: why does it matter for us? Or to say it differently, why is it better news than what we talked about above?

I genuinely believe the gospel is the best story ever told, but we've lost what made it good. And I think that's because our gospel no longer looks like Jesus or sounds like the good news stories he told. A few years ago, I heard a very prominent pastor say, "Jesus never preached the gospel," which is a wild thing to say. How can we believe that the person who is the center of our faith and the subject of the gospel never talked about it? I disagree with this pastor—I think the gospel is the primary thing Jesus talked about—but I do agree with him that our modern gospel stories look very little like the stories Jesus told. And I believe that that often causes fragmentation in our spiritual lives.

Many of us love Jesus and are compelled by his words, but when we look at our modern gospel stories, theologies, and traditions we don't see him reflected. The stories we tell are all about going to heaven when we die or dealing with a vindictive judge, and rarely if ever speak to life here and now. Our modern gospel may offer forgiveness from sins, but as the couple who met with me articulated, has nothing to do with the sins of systemic racism or injustice. Is that really all our gospel offers? Is that the extent of good news? What about Jesus' teaching on enemy love? What about Jesus' confrontation of religious leaders? What about the way Jesus protected women from public shame? Or the way Jesus sought out and touched differently abled and disabled bodies who had been outcast from society? Is that not gospel? I believe that is exactly what the gospel is.

Jesus is the very center of the gospel. When Jesus confronts, heals, welcomes, and protects, we are seeing the gospel in action—the good news in the flesh. And when Jesus teaches his disciples, telling them stories about elaborate parties, upside-down kingdoms, and reunited families, he is connecting his actions with his purpose. He is preaching the gospel. The good news about good news is that it looks and sounds like Jesus.

PRODIGAL GOSPEL

The goal of this book is to help us rediscover the good news according to Jesus. To do that, we are going to look at one of Jesus' stories. It is the longest and arguably most famous of all of Jesus' parables. You probably know this story by its popular name, the parable of the prodigal son.

Theologians and Bible scholars have often referred to the parable of the prodigal son as the "gospel in a nutshell."[2] Jesus tells this story to explain to his fiercest critics what he was doing and why. As we read this parable we are hearing, in Jesus' own words, the good news of the gospel. It's like the lead writer, actor, and director of a movie telling us what the story is about. In the same way, the gospel is the story Jesus is writing, acting in, and directing. When we listen to Jesus tell the parable of the prodigal son, we are hearing the good news from the one who is *Goodnews*.

If we want to rediscover the good news of the gospel, we need to listen—*really* listen—to Jesus tell it and allow his gospel to challenge, enlarge, and renew our current understanding. This is his news to tell, and if our version doesn't look like his, something is amiss.

In the pages to come we will dive into Jesus' parable of the prodigal son. We'll explore the context, history, and characters to see how this story offers us good news today. Then we will zoom out to see how the "gospel in a nutshell" reveals the gospel in large, like a good news pattern that we can trace throughout God's larger story. In the last two chapters, we will see how Jesus' story is an invitation into a living reality, here and now.

I love this story. Every time I read it, I'm caught by surprise. It's funny, disarming, moving, and incredibly challenging. It continues to restore my faith when I experience fragmentation and deconstruction. As you read this book, I pray that you too are surprised, disarmed, and challenged by the wildly good news of Jesus. Maybe you're like my friend Kev, suffering under the weight of a terrifying story. I pray Jesus' words would be a tender word of love and welcome. Maybe you're frustrated with the gap between gospel and life. I pray Jesus' word would pull together the pieces of your fragmented faith into something new and empowering. Maybe you're like the couple who don't see the connection between Jesus and the destructive and painful systems of the world.

I pray the Jesus story would enlarge your gospel to make it good news for the whole world. Jesus told this story to a diverse crowd of cynics, skeptics, haters, followers, and the curious. No matter who you are or where you're coming from, I believe this story is for you.

QUESTIONS

After each chapter, I'll provide a few questions for reflection and a prayer. We're just getting started, so we will keep things brief here.

1. As you begin this book, can you name how you're feeling about faith and the gospel?

2. How would you define or explain the gospel to someone? In this chapter, we explored how the gospel is the good news that Jesus came to reveal something about God and accomplish God's purposes. Would you take a moment to write out what you believe . . .

   a. Jesus reveals?

   b. Jesus accomplishes?

   c. And what makes that good news?

Prayer
God of *good news*, help us hear the story you're telling.

Amen.

ONE

Prodigal Gospel

THROUGHOUT COLLEGE I worked at a little coffee shop in the corner of a suburban strip mall between a Gold's Gym and a tanning salon. Nearly every day a man would come in carrying a Bible and a chessboard. He would sit by himself, quietly reading, until someone would ask him about either the Bible or the chessboard. Coffee shops are interesting that way—they encourage strange interactions and make space for relationships that would be hard to find anywhere else. The man was friendly, generous, and funny. People loved to sit with him and talk. They'd ask him questions, make jokes, debate faith, and always play chess.

When the chessboard came out, the man would propose a wager: "If you beat me, I'll buy you a drink. But if I win, I get to tell you about Jesus." People loved it, especially young men, and they'd take him up on it again and again. Sometimes he'd play chess for hours, rotating through a group of guys eager to prove their intellect. But here's the secret: he was very good at chess. In high school he'd been the captain of his chess team and now, thanks to his wager, he got to practice his game for hours a day. I'm not sure anyone ever beat him.

I watched it happen dozens of times from behind the counter. Full of gusto, men would challenge him to a game of chess and each time, often quickly, they'd find themselves in checkmate. The game was over, they'd lost. They knew it, he knew it, I knew it from the behind the counter. But then, the man would do something they did not expect. He'd take the board and turn it 180 degrees, so that his well-played game was now theirs. He'd then look at them and say, "You won! Let me buy you a drink." Which he did, and then, he'd tell them about Jesus.

The man would compare his opponent's life to a game of chess, a game they could never win. You make a move, he would explain, but God makes the better move until you come to the end of your life—the game—and find yourself in checkmate to God. What does God do? He switches places with you, he turns the chessboard around so that his well-played game can be yours. He, in Jesus, lived perfectly in all the ways you did not. He played the perfect game and now gives it to you, a sort of substitutionary victory. Through Jesus, you get his well-earned life, his victory, and the prize of eternal life. What a game.

PRODIGAL GOSPEL

There are, basically, two ways to talk about the gospel. The first way is to describe what the gospel is and does with theological statements, like "Jesus died on the cross for our sins," or by using religious terms like *salvation* and *justification*. These are important ways of talking about the gospel, which we will do in this chapter and throughout this book. The second way to talk about the gospel is with stories, metaphors, and images. The chess game is a metaphor for the gospel. Instead of diving into specific minutiae, we use a story to capture the essence and flow of the gospel. When I started writing this book I asked friends, family, and even strangers how they first heard the gospel, and nearly every time they responded with a story and not a list of statements or theological ideas.

Gospel stories are powerful because they condense intricacies and abstractions into something relatable. We may not grasp why or how Jesus' death deals with sin, but we can understand a father who will give anything to reunite with a child. And we don't often use words like *atonement* or *salvation*, but we can get our hearts around dinner parties and family reunions. That's one of the reasons Jesus told so many parables. His little stories help us see something bigger.

We tell stories to help us understand the truth of the gospel, but those stories also shape and inform how we think about the gospel. Stories provide emotion and color. Think of how music in a movie sets the tone—depending on the music, a scene can feel dramatic or comedic, heartwarming or heartbreaking. Stories, especially the ones we use to tell the gospel, do the same thing. A story about a chess match emphasizes something different than a story about a father who searches for lost sons, or a story about a woman who stops everything to find a missing coin. Each of these is a gospel story, but they are not the same in either what they communicate about the gospel or how they communicate it.

That leads us back to the chess match. I love this story and my friend who tells it, but I think it illustrates a problem so many of our gospel stories have. The problem is how the chess match represents you, me, the world, and God. We can summarize the problem in one question: Why are we playing a game against God?

THE BRIDGE

Right before I started writing this chapter, I had dinner with some friends who, for a few summers, worked as counselors at a Christian camp. The camp was run by a large Christian organization and trained counselors to present the gospel in a very specific way. While having dinner, I asked my friends what image came to mind when they the thought about the gospel and with a laugh they both said, "The bridge!"

"The bridge" is a visual story of the gospel, a way to illustrate what Jesus accomplished on the cross and why it matters, and the camp counselors were taught to draw it out as they talked. In the picture you see two cliffs, separated by a chasm in the middle. On the left we stand in sin, death, and condemnation. On the right, we find God and the hope of eternal life, forgiveness, and relationship. The issue is the gap separating us from God. The divide is too great for us to cross; we cannot, on our own, make our way to God. Some versions of "the bridge" illustration include visuals of us trying to build a bridge with good works, moral behavior, and accomplishments, to show that no matter how hard we try, we are incapable of bridging the gap between God and us. What are we to do? Nothing—we cannot get to God. The good news is that Jesus, through the cross, makes a way for us to get to God. Through his death and resurrection, we are forgiven and made righteous so that we can "*cross* the bridge" (get it?) and get to God.

Like the chess match, the bridge is another gospel story we use to condense the intricacies of the gospel into something relatable and approachable. The central premise of the bridge is that we are separated from God. We sinned, alienating ourselves from God and our true home. This is in part true—in the pages to come we'll talk about the prodigal son, who is the archetypal example of someone leaving home and separating themselves from God. Here's the rub though: the bridge implies that God is also separated from us. According to this idea, God had to turn away from us when we sinned. Thus, the gap represents our sin *and* God's choice to move away, separate from, and leave us. This story has a similar tone to the chess match; for whatever reason, God is not with us. God is on the other side of the chessboard, or across the gap, and either will not or cannot cross the divide or flip the chessboard and end the game altogether.

Some might protest at this point and say, "Yes, but Jesus!" And it's true. Jesus is God with us. In the chess match, Jesus gives us his well-played game, and in the bridge, Jesus crosses the divide so that we can cross it in turn. Those are both beautiful pictures that do tell us something true, but they each lead to more questions about our gospel. Like, where was Jesus before his incarnation, crucifixion, resurrection, and ascension? Why did God stay separate from us for so long? Why, at any moment, were we playing a game against God? It feels like an incongruous picture. One moment we're separated from God, and then Jesus crosses the divide. One moment, we're playing against God, but now God's game is ours. It almost feels like God is divided against Godself. Is Jesus for us but God against us?

SURVEY RESULTS

Have you heard stories like these? I grew up in the evangelical church but didn't hear these gospel stories until college. That doesn't mean I never heard any gospel stories, just not these ones. When I was in middle school, I learned how to share my faith using *tracts,* little religious pamphlets that often include some kind of clever question, image, or story that was intended to lead a person into a gospel conversation. (As a weird aside, I got most of the tracts from a ministry run by the kid from *Growing Pains.*) Some of the tracts looked like a fake million-dollar bill, some like the beginning of a close-up magic act, and others like a zine a local artist would have put together. But the tract I remember using the most was a survey. On its surface it looked benign, but as you kept working through the survey, the questions shifted to:

"Do you consider yourself a good person?"

"Have you ever lied? Even a little white lie counts."

"Have you ever stolen? Even something small."

"Have you ever felt jealousy? Maybe for your neighbor's house or stuff."

"Have you ever felt hate towards someone?"

The answer to these questions is *yes.* That's the point of the survey. And when a participant would say yes, you'd respond saying something like:

"Well, Jerry based on your own admission you're a lying, thieving, coveting, and murderous person because according to Jesus, to hate a person is to have committed murder. Therefore, according to you, you've broken at least four of God commands. So, do you still think you're a good person? If you were to die today do you think you'd go to heaven? Well do you, Jerry?"

It's not a great way to start a relationship, but the purpose of the survey was to *lead* people into the recognition that they were very bad and needed to be forgiven by Jesus. It's a trap, designed to produce a very specific result. It's not curious, humble, or thoughtful. That doesn't mean no one has had a meaningful experience using these tracts, but they're designed to ignore complexity so that even me, a weird thirteen-year-old, could administer them and hopefully lead people to accept Jesus as their personal Lord and Savior, as the only way they could be saved from their life of *murder*.

Is that really the good news of the gospel? The survey, the chess match, and the gap are different ways of telling the gospel story, but if I can be honest with you, none of them sound like good news. I have a lot of problems with these versions of the gospel, which we'll explore in the pages to come. But if I was to boil it all down into one idea it would be this: this version of God doesn't seem very good. In each story, God is oppositional—playing a game against us, separating from us, or counting all our sins to trap us. There's a kind of rescue in each story, but one that ignores the complexity and problems we experience in our world and lives. Why doesn't God stop the chess match if God is all powerful? Why doesn't God jump over the ravine right away? Why do none of these stories offer good news to the world? And why does God make such fearful ultimatums?

Growing up in the American church, these are the kinds of questions that began to fester in me. When I read the Bible and looked at Jesus, I saw a story that seemed so much bigger and better than the ones offered by our little gospel stories. And when I look at my life and the world, I must admit that we need a better story than the one our little gospels offer.

Here's the good news: the gospel is bigger and better than our little stories represent. The rest of this book is about showing you what I mean. But before we go much further, I think we need to zoom out a bit and ask ourselves, what is the gospel? And then we can ask, how did Jesus tell the gospel? Does his story look like ours? I can tell you right now the answer is no—his story is much better.

WHAT IS THE GOSPEL?

So, what is the gospel? Let's begin with a simple definition. The gospel is a story. That's literally what the word means. *Gospel* comes from the Anglo-Saxon word *godspell,* which translates to "good story," but we can trace the word all the way back through the Latin to the Greek word *euangelion,* which means "good news." I love the word *godspell,* partly because I'll always be a theater kid at heart, but more importantly because "good story" is what the gospel is supposed to be. But gospel doesn't refer to just any good story. When Jesus and the biblical writers used the word *gospel* (*euangelion*) to describe Jesus' work, they were borrowing a word with history. In the ancient world, *gospel* was reserved to announce big, world-changing stories, like a wedding, the birth of a child, or even the end of war. When the writers of the New Testament use the word *gospel,* they're telling us to pay attention, because this is a "good news" kind of story.

So the gospel is a story, but what is the story about? The best place to find our answer is to look at the four books that come at the beginning of the New Testament, dubbed "the Gospels." This is such an intuitive place to begin that it almost feels counterintuitive, but these four books record the gospel. Today we talk about the four Gospels as though they are a kind of literary genre, but when they were first penned, they were simply called "the Gospel" and no one referred to them in the plural until a century after they were written.[1] Early Christians simply called these four books, "the Gospel according to" Matthew, Mark, Luke, and John because they believed each of these Gospels told the very same gospel story. As New Testament scholar Scot McKnight writes, "[Early Christians] called these books 'the Gospels' because they are the gospel."[2] And what are the Gospels about? McKnight goes on to say, "The Gospels are about Jesus, they tell the Story of Jesus, and everything in them is about Jesus. . . . The evangelists (notice what we call them!) were telling the Story of Jesus as the gospel because it was the gospel."[3]

What is the gospel? It is the story of Jesus. We'll explore what that means in a moment, but I don't want to skip past this too quickly. The gospel is the *story of Jesus*. And this describes not just the chapters that include his death or resurrection, though those moments are crucial components of the gospel. His whole story is the gospel. From announcement to ascension, from his first cry to his last sigh, from the wedding at Cana to the wedding feast of the Lamb, it's all his story and all good news. If we want to know, understand, and experience the good news of the gospel, then we need to look to Jesus and his story. Not just one moment but all of it and how it all fits together. We need to hear what Jesus says and watch how he loves. We need to see him throw dinner parties for the estranged and watch him confront the proud. We need to pay attention as he kneels to wash feet and follow him across the barriers imposed by religion and misogyny. If we want to know the gospel, we need to look at Jesus.

GOOD STORIES VS. GOOD NEWS

The gospel is the story of Jesus. This is a good place to begin. But as we've already seen, gospel is more than a story, it's good news. Most people I meet, even those who don't identify as Christian, think Jesus' story was good. It's hard not to, because Jesus was a compelling figure. I was recently talking to an ex-Mormon who is now an atheist passionately opposed to the Mormon Church, but in our conversation, he made it abundantly clear that he wasn't opposed to Jesus. The more we talked, the more he shared his deep admiration for Jesus. He loved Jesus' teachings and thought that religion had gone astray by losing Jesus, which I totally agree with. It's rare I meet someone who doesn't think Jesus was great. People are often critical of all the things that have come to be associated with Jesus, but Jesus—they're into him.

Thinking Jesus' story is good is different than believing it's good news. Being good news means the story has an impact on the world. It announces something, changes something, and means something for you and me. Jesus confronting the religious leaders for their exclusionary and oppressive practices is a good story, but what makes it good news? And Jesus comforting the estranged and partying with outcasts is a good story, but what makes it good news? How do those realities change us? What do they mean for us? Let's look at three big ways Jesus' story becomes good news.

JESUS REVEALS WHAT GOD IS LIKE

The first way Jesus' story becomes good news is that Jesus reveals God. The gospel according to John begins with this beautiful introduction where the author writes, "No one has ever seen God. God the only Son, who is at the Father's side, *has made God known*" (John 1:18, italics mine). Similarly, in Colossians, a letter written by the apostle Paul, we read, "The Son is the *image of the invisible God*" (Colossians 1:15, italics mine). Look at that again: Jesus "has made God known," and Jesus is "the image of the invisible God." When we look at Jesus, we're seeing a picture of God. And yes, that's because Jesus is God, but Jesus is also revealing what God is like. The good news about Jesus is that he reveals what God is like.

In Jesus, the image of the invisible God, we get a perfect picture of God's nature and character. *God is just like Jesus.* The author of Hebrews makes this same point, saying,

> In the past God spoke to our ancestors through the prophets at many times and in various ways, but in these last days he has spoken to us by his Son, whom he appointed heir of all things, and through whom also he made the universe. The Son is the radiance of God's glory *and the exact representation* of his being. (Hebrews 1:1–3 NIV, italics mine)

The good news of Jesus' story is that God is just like Jesus. As we watch Jesus teach, heal, and eat with outcasts, we are seeing the "exact representation" of God. When Jesus confronts the religious leaders for exploiting their position, we're seeing the "image of the invisible God" confront oppressive religious institutions. When Jesus includes women in his inner circle, we're seeing God upend systemic barriers to inclusion. In Jesus we see what God is like, what God wants, and what God does. As Jesus himself said, "Whatever the Father does, the Son does likewise" (John 5:19).

God is like Jesus, and the writer of 1 John tells us explicitly what this means about God: "This is how the love of God is revealed to us: God has sent his only Son into the world so that we can live through him" (1 John 4:9). The author then goes on to add the most important definitional characteristic of God, that "God is love" (1 John 4:16). In Jesus, we see a perfect revelation of God; an image of other-oriented sacrificial love. This is who God is. There are no ifs, ands, or buts about it. God is love, God is like Jesus. That's the gospel.

I honestly believe this is the most important thing I can tell you. If you stopped reading here, I'd be a little bummed, but at least you would have heard this: God is just like Jesus. I don't know what tradition you grew up in. I don't know how you imagine God or what you've been told God is like. But here's the thing: God is like Jesus, and all our other images, theologies, or ideas about God must get squared with Jesus, not the other way around. No other teaching or even scripture gets priority over our image of God—it all comes to Jesus. As the author of Hebrews said, "In the past God spoke to our ancestors through the prophets," but now "he has spoken to us by his Son," who is the perfect and ultimate word from and image of God.

JESUS IS WHAT GOD IS UP TO

The second way Jesus' story is good news is that he shows us what God is up to. At the beginning of his ministry, after forty days in the wilderness, Jesus went to his hometown synagogue in Nazareth to make a big announcement, sort of like a presidential candidate returning to their home state to announce the beginning of their campaign. At the synagogue, Jesus took a scroll that contained the writings of the prophet Isaiah.

He unrolled the scroll and found the place where it was written:

The Spirit of the Lord is upon me,
    because the Lord has anointed me.
He has sent me to preach good news [gospel] to the poor,
    to proclaim release to the prisoners

and recovery of sight to the blind,
to liberate the oppressed,
and to proclaim the year of the Lord's favor.

He rolled up the scroll, gave it back to the synagogue assistant, and sat down. Every eye in the synagogue was fixed on him. He began to explain to them, "Today, this scripture has been fulfilled just as you heard it." (Luke 4:17–21, addition mine)

To understand what's happening, we need a bit of context. The prophet Isaiah was talking about an important event in the life of ancient Israel called Jubilee—a legal provision given by God to Israel to create rhythms of redemption and restoration. Every fifty years debts would be canceled, slaves set free, and lost property returned. Jubilee was called "the year of the Lord's favor" because it was about experiencing abundance and redemption. If you had been cut off from your family, Jubilee was about reunion. If your grandfather had been swindled out of the family farm, Jubilee was about putting an end to cycles of poverty by returning you to your ancestral land. If you worked every day without ever receiving a break, Jubilee was about rest and giving you and your land a chance to recover. In a word, Jubilee was about restoration. It was about setting things right and making families, communities, environments, and people whole.

Jubilee was a beautiful idea, but sadly, there's no evidence Israel ever practiced it. Instead of practicing Jubilee, Israel acted like all the other nations around them. An elite few grew increasingly wealthy, the poor were exploited, the land overtaxed, and with time the nation drifted away from God. Jubilee became a dream. A dream maintained by the prophets and poets of Israel, like Isaiah, who longed for a day when God would step into time and space and bring about an even greater kind of Jubilee that not only addressed the needs of the poor but revitalized the heart of the nation. This hope grew in the life of Israel as they suffered under the weight of history. Nation after nation conquered Israel and each time, the hope of Jubilee took on more significance.

That is what makes this moment from Luke 4 so important. In using this passage from Isaiah to announce his public work, Jesus was connecting his story to the ancient hope of Israel and declaring to everyone listening, *I am here to fulfill this promise and bring about Jubilee—the restoration of all things.* This is how Jesus begins his public ministry, this is his campaign announcement, his inaugural address—I don't think we can overstate how important this is. Argentinian theologian Esteban Voth calls Jesus' gospel proclamation here "the Great Omission," because we so often skip over it when talking about the gospel and move directly to issues like sin, heaven, and life after death.[4] But that's not where Jesus began. Jesus began with Jubilee, restoration, and the fulfillment of Israel's ancient hopes.

At the same time, Jesus' Jubilee was bigger than just Israel's hopes. After Jesus read from Isaiah, the crowds were "raving about Jesus, so impressed were they by the gracious words flowing from his lips" (Luke 4:22). But then Jesus does something they do not like; he tells two stories from the Old Testament that center on non-Israelites experiencing restoration. Watch how the crowd's enthusiasm flips: "When they heard this, everyone in the synagogue was filled with anger. They rose up and ran him out of town. They led him to the crest of the hill on which their town had been built so that they could throw him off the cliff" (Luke 4:28–29). Jesus took the ancient hope of Israel and expanded it to include all the world. He was showing them, and us, that God is for us and our neighbors, friends, and even enemies.

JESUS INVITES US TO PARTICIPATE WITH HIM

Finally, our last big idea that makes the gospel good news is that Jesus invites us to participate with him in his life, work, and way—here and now. The good news of Jesus is not just something that happens to us or around us, it is something we're invited into. When Jesus said "Follow me" to his disciples, he was inviting them to experience, live, and participate in the good news story he was living. We see this explicitly after Jesus washes his disciples' feet. Look at what he says:

> After he washed the disciples' feet, he put on his robes and returned to his place at the table. He said to them, "Do you know what I've done for you? You call me 'Teacher' and 'Lord,' and you speak correctly, because I am. If I, your Lord and teacher, have washed your feet, you too must wash each other's feet. I have given you an example: Just as I have done, you also must do." (John 13:12–15)

Jesus is saying, if you believe I am who I say I am, then do as I do. A little later, Jesus adds, "I give you a new commandment: Love each other. Just as I have loved you, so you also must love each other" (John 13:34). The gospel is an invitation to experience the love of Jesus and to partner with Jesus in loving like he does.

This is one of the biggest holes in our modern understanding of the gospel. Our gospel stories tend to focus on forgiveness of sins and life after death with little to nothing offered to life here and now. But Jesus' emphasis is on living his story, now. In him, we're invited to know and experience the love of God, now. In him, we are invited to extend restoration to the world around us, now. In him, we are invited to partner together and live a new story, now. In him, we are invited to participate in our own healing, now. The gospel is good news for here and now.

SUMMARY

We've covered a lot of ground, so let's pause here for a moment to review. So far, we've said:

- The gospel is the story of Jesus.

- The gospel is good news that God is just like Jesus.

- The gospel is good news that Jesus is restoring all things.

- The gospel is good news that we're invited to participate in the life of Jesus, here and now.

- Amen.

Maybe you're wondering where ideas like sin, atonement, or salvation fit. In the following chapters we'll explore these ideas and more, but I believe that to understand any of the "Christianese" words we associate with gospel we must begin with the revelation, restoration, and invitation of God in Jesus. We must begin with Jesus.

The biggest problems our gospel has today is that it does not begin with Jesus. We skip Jesus and jump straight to theological concepts like justification. But the problem is, justification only makes sense in Jesus. To try and read someone like the apostle Paul without Jesus at the center is to misread the apostle Paul altogether. Jesus is the center, subject, and object of the gospel. The gospel is the good news about Jesus. When we miss how Jesus talked about the gospel, we risk displacing Jesus altogether. But when we begin with Jesus, we see how his entire life, all the writings of the Bible, and even our own work today makes sense in him.

VIBE CHECK

Now, what does any of this have to do with the parable of the prodigal son? That's a great question, thanks for asking. Let's return to our earlier conversation about the stories, images, and metaphors we use to tell the gospel. These little stories help us compress theological details into something understandable and relatable. We talked about two such stories—the bridge and the chess match—both of which are understandable and relatable but also fail to capture the vibe and content of the gospel. First we can look at content: neither mentions Jesus revealing God. Both include a kind of restoration, but neither show how the gospel offers anything to the world around us. There's an invitation, but not much about life, here and now.

But they're also missing the vibe of the gospel. I know *vibe* isn't a very technical word, and maybe it feels irrelevant to you. I can imagine someone protesting my use of the word *vibe* by saying something like, "Vibe is irrelevant to truth." And at one level I agree with that. Some things are true whether I like the vibe or not. For example, it's true that Madonna tried to remake *Casablanca* with Ashton Kutcher. That's not good, but it is true. Some things are like that—unavoidable truths. And yet, at the same time, how we say something impacts how we are heard. That's why the stories we use to tell the gospel are important—they communicate truth but also tenor. They should help us understand that the gospel is both true and good. That's what I mean by vibe.

The chess match and the gap both have the vibe of the gospel all wrong. The tone doesn't match the truth. Both stories position God in opposition to humanity. We are on one side of the chessboard and God is on the other. We are on one side of the chasm, and God is on the other. And yes, in these stories God rectifies the situation by switching places with us or bridging the gap, but why are we playing a game against God in the first place? Why did God leave us on this side of the chasm for so long? Why didn't God come over to us and fix the world instead of ferrying us to the other side? That's not good or true.

The good news of the gospel is that God is just like Jesus, who is resorting all things and inviting all of us into his life right now. I believe that is both a more Jesus-centered, biblical, apostolic articulation of the gospel, and simply a better story. Both matter, because the gospel is supposed to be good and true. A story so good it must be true.

THE GOSPEL ACCORDING TO JESUS

Here is how all of this connects to the parable of the prodigal son: Jesus told this story to communicate the truth and goodness of the gospel. He told it in response to a group of religious leaders who were complaining about his work—the gospel. It's his way of compressing the theological minutiae of his broader story into something relatable and understandable. It can be hard to wrap your mind around the love of God, but it's a bit easier to get your heart around the love of a father who will pay any price to be reunited with his boy. Restoration and Jubilee are big ideas, but I think every one of us knows the longing and joy of holding someone you love after they've been away. And the invitation to participate in the life of Christ might feel abstract, but there's a good chance you've been to a party that got a little wild.

If you haven't read the parable of the prodigal son in a while, now would be a good time to go review it. You can find it in Luke 15; I suggest reading the entire chapter, because the prodigal son parable is the climactic end of a series of three stories. Some English Bibles divide the three stories with individual headers, but the original manuscripts place them together because they are all unified by a similar theme, or vibe. The Common English Bible, the translation I use throughout most of this book, keeps them together under the single heading "occasions for celebration." I absolutely love that single heading, because "celebration" might be the best word to describe the vibe of Jesus' gospel. Where the gap, the chess match, or the survey present God in opposition to humanity, Jesus' stories represent God as a good father who wants to celebrate with his kids. Jesus' God isn't distanced or separated from us; he's not scowling at us from the other side of a cliff or making calculated moves like an opponent in an ill-fated chess match. Instead, he's scanning the horizon for signs of his kids so that he can lay the table, light the barbecue, and crank the music to eleven.

And the vibe of Jesus' parable matches the message of the gospel. This short little story shows us revelation, restoration, and invitation. The father is a revelation of God—in other words, this is Jesus' own understanding of God—and the story is saturated in the language of other-oriented love. When the youngest son returns and when the father goes searching for the oldest, we see a glimpse of restoration. The youngest is returned to a place of honor and sonship, and the oldest is invited into restored relationship with his younger. And at the center of the parable is a party, a window into participation in the life of Christ here and now.

The parable of the prodigal son is the gospel in a nutshell, containing both the truth and goodness of the Jesus story. The truth looks like what we've sketched here: revelation, restoration, and invitation. The parable doesn't contain every detail that we could include within the gospel, but it distills the essential truths. And I think, just as importantly, the parable of the prodigal son gets the vibe right. The medium matches the message. Or to say it another way, the story looks like Jesus, who is the gospel.

Throughout the rest of this book, we're going to dance between the specifics of the parable and the broader story of the gospel. This chapter was just the beginning. We have outlined what the gospel is and why the parable matters, but throughout the rest of this book my goal is to show it to you. I hope to tell you both the truth and the goodness of the gospel, to communicate both the vibe and the vision.

QUESTIONS

1. Before reading this chapter, how would you have described or explained the gospel? Would you have used a theological statement or told a story?

2. Would you consider your answer to the first question a good news story? What makes it feel like good news or, if it is not, what makes you uneasy about that version of the gospel?

3. How does Jesus compare to your images of God? Does it feel like good news that God looks and acts like Jesus, or does it provoke something different within you?

4. How do the ideas of revelation, restoration, and invitation challenge, expand, or impact your previous understanding of the gospel?

5. Are there any questions about the gospel you feel haven't been addressed yet?

Prayer

God, who is love, help us recover the good news of your story. Once upon a time, people were set alight by the glory of your love. But today it can feel like we're far removed from what made it all good. Please give us ears to hear, eyes to see, and hearts to receive the vast expanse of your goodness. May we be confronted and comforted by your revelation, set free by your restoration, and empowered by your invitation.

Amen.

TWO

Prodigal Son, Part 1

Jesus said, "A certain man had two sons. The younger son said to his father, 'Father, give me my share of the inheritance.' Then the father divided his estate between them. Soon afterward, the younger son gathered everything together and took a trip to a land far away. There, he wasted his wealth through extravagant living.

"When he had used up his resources, a severe food shortage arose in that country and he began to be in need. He hired himself out to one of the citizens of that country, who sent him into his fields to feed pigs. He longed to eat his fill from what the pigs ate, but no one gave him anything. When he came to his senses, he said, 'How many of my father's hired hands have more than enough food, but I'm starving to death! I will get up and go to my father, and say to him, "Father, I have sinned against heaven and against you. I no longer deserve to be called your son. Take me on as one of your hired hands."' So he got up and went to his father.

"While he was still a long way off, his father saw him and was moved with compassion. His father ran to him, hugged him, and kissed him. Then his son said, 'Father, I have sinned against heaven and against you. I no longer deserve to be called your son.' But the father said to his servants, 'Quickly, bring out the best robe and put it on him! Put a ring on his finger and sandals on his feet! Fetch the fattened calf and slaughter it. We must celebrate with feasting because this son of mine was dead and has come back to life! He was lost and is found!' And they began to celebrate." (Luke 15:11–24)

I can only remember telling my stepdad "You're not my real dad" once. I know I said it other times, it was an easy jab, but I only *really* remember saying it once. Sometimes memory is like that—one image distills the weight of a thousand tiny moments. It was a long time ago, but remembering it today still brings a twinge of shame and embarrassment—there are few things more cringe than nineties teen angst. But I think the real reason I remember the moment is because of how my dad responded. Shouting "you're not my real dad" was meant to provoke him. It was an insult intended to sting, to hurt, and to start a fight. But instead of responding in kind, my dad was calm. I don't really remember what he said, but I do remember how it made me feel. My words felt hollow. It was like my dad's serenity exposed a lie. I wanted rage. I wanted a confirmation of all the painful things I was feeling. I wanted him to say, "You're right, no one cares." But he didn't. All I remember him saying was, "I am," and then he sat there with me until I couldn't bear it anymore and I got up and left.

I've been thinking back on this memory because of how Jesus began the parable of the prodigal son. Saying "You're not my real dad" is not a one-for-one comparison to the actions of the younger son, but my story makes me wonder about the internal motivations of the son. What did he want? Did he want to wound, to insult, to provoke? And what did he expect his father to do? Did he expect rage? Did he want confirmation of some painful story he'd been telling himself? And how did he feel when, instead of rage, the father consented? Was his father's calm as confrontational to him as mine was to me? Is that why he left?

Jesus doesn't answer any of these questions. And this is a parable, not a history. But I can't help but ask these questions, probably because I see myself as a prodigal son, but also because this parable is a metaphor for our *real* relationship with God, self, and others. When Jesus chooses to explain the gospel, he uses a story about the relationship of a father to his sons. And that's important to pay attention to because often, when talking about the gospel, our language is less relational and more transactional. We talk about sin as "bad actions" or "violations of the law" through which we accrue guilt or debt before God. To save us, Jesus pays the penalty for our sin, sort of like paying off our debt, so that we can be forgiven and go to heaven. That's transactional language.

But here's what's interesting about Jesus' story: even though money is involved, Jesus is uninterested in focusing on a transaction. Instead, everything in this story is relational. The wound, the fracture, and the repair are all described in relational ways. Debt and guilt take a back seat to issues like estrangement and disconnection. At one moment in the story, the father even refuses to enter a transactional negotiation with his son. It seems that what Jesus cares about and what Jesus wants us to see is the relational heart of God and of the gospel.

So, even though telling my stepdad he wasn't my real dad is not a direct comparison to the story of the prodigal son, maybe it is even closer than I first realized. Maybe the issues at the heart of the gospel aren't debt, guilt, penalties, or violations of the law but relationships, wounds, and disconnection. Maybe the questions are about the stories we tell ourselves, the response we expect, and the peace we're met with. And maybe, just maybe, the good news is less about a transaction and more about restoration.

A CONVOLUTED STORY

Jesus begins his story with a strange scenario. Here is how it begins: a youngest son comes to his father and demands his inheritance. Every sermon I've heard about this parable talks about how wrong this request is—inheritances, normally, are distributed after death. But here's where things get complicated—the youngest son's request is offensive, but it's not technically wrong. There is no law or rule in Torah (Israel's religious and national law) that prohibits a child from asking for their inheritance. We could argue that it's impudent and petulant. We could say it's irresponsible and reckless. But it's not, in a technical sense, wrong. However, it is wrong in a relational way. In demanding his inheritance from his father, the youngest son is, in effect, telling his dad that he wishes he were dead. That he values his father's stuff more than he values his father's life. And that's a different kind of wrong. The kind that hurts and harms. The kind that wounds. Like telling a man who loves you he's not your real dad, it's not against the law, but it is against *him*. And that's something deeper and more painful than a violation of the law—it's a violation of relationship.

Jesus is constantly challenging folks to think bigger than the law. Or it might be more accurate to say he challenges people to see what the law was intended for. When asked what the most important command was, Jesus responded by saying, love God and love others as you love yourself (Matthew 22:36–40). In saying this, he took the 613 commands of the Old Testament law and boiled them down to two. Then, near the end of his time on earth, Jesus simplified things even further, saying, "I give you a new commandment: Love each other. Just as I have loved you, so you also must love each other" (John 13:34). It's not that the law was bad or unimportant, but its true purpose was love. And when love was lost as the central and defining reality of the law, the law lost its purpose. That's why Jesus confronted the religious leaders saying things like, "How terrible it will be for you legal experts and Pharisees! Hypocrites! You give to God a tenth of mint, dill, and cumin, but you forget about the more important matters of the Law: justice, peace, and faith" (Matthew 23:23). The religious leaders followed the law to the letter but missed its purpose.

Similarly, the parable of the prodigal son is meant to reorder our perspective. The issue here isn't violations of the law but violations of relationship. In a way, the younger son is following the letter of the law because his demand isn't against the law. If all that matters is the law, then he can make this demand and wipe his hands clean of any wrongdoing. But Jesus is drawing our attention away from legalism towards relationality. He's showing us that what matters is how we love. You can follow the law and hurt one another. You can keep every rule and regulation and still be a jerk.

THE FLIP SIDE

Now here is where things get interesting. It's not that the Old Testament law had nothing to say about this scenario. The son's request is *technically* legal, but it could be considered a violation of other components of the law if the father chose to press charges. Here's what I mean: In Deuteronomy 21, we have a really fun (just to be clear, that's a joke) passage that gives parents permission to bring a "consistently stubborn" child (Deuteronomy 21:18) before the elders of a village to charge them and stone them (verse 21).

If the father wanted to, he could do this. If the father perceived his son's actions as stubborn, he could have pressed charges. The ancient Near Eastern world was a patriarchal society in which fathers virtually owned their children, meaning society was already inclined towards the father. And the father could make a pretty compelling argument that his son was stubborn and refused to "listen to [his] father or mother" (verse 18), which are the grounds necessary for stoning. But he doesn't. Where the law could be applied, it's not. Instead, the father consents to his son's request and allows him to leave with his share of the inheritance. Where he could condemn, legislate, and judge, the father gives. Where he could wield the law like a hammer, the father ignores it. Where he could, at the very least, strike the boy across the face for his insolence, the father chooses to absorb the painful request into himself and protect his son from the penalty of the law.

Sometimes our gospel presentation makes God beholden to the law. We say things like, the law is an expression of God's perfect nature and therefore, for God to be holy and just, God *must* judge sin according to the law. But in Jesus' story, the father, who represents God, chooses to ignore the law to protect his son. That's because God is not beholden to the law, the law is beholden to God. This is important to get our minds around, because later we will talk about Jesus' death on the cross. And when our gospel is legalistic and transactional, we make Jesus' death a sacrifice to pay back the debt incurred by our violations of the law. In this way, the law becomes the ultimate and final arbiter that must be satisfied. But the law is not God. God is. And the God we see displayed in this parable, and in Jesus, is the God of noncoercive, sacrificial, other-oriented love.

Instead of wielding the law against his son, the father chooses to consent to his request. The father divides up his estate and gives the requisite portion to his youngest son. Later in the story, we'll learn how upset this makes the older brother. In the brother's mind, the father is funding the misadventure of the younger son. And in a way he is. The father takes a risk here, a sort of calculated gamble in love. He could try to compel or even coerce his son to stay, but coercion never produces love. So instead the father grants his son the dignity of choice and freedom. That's not an easy gift. A New Testament scholar, Kenneth Bailey, writes, "It is out of the father's costly love that he grants the request. In the process the father grants the ultimate form of freedom, namely the freedom to reject the offered relationship."[1] The father gives his son the choice to reject him.

That's what love does. Real love can't make ultimatums or hold someone hostage. Real love is self-sacrificial and other-oriented, empowering the agency of another. And it's a risk. The son may choose to reject the father. He may walk away and never come back. And yet it is a calculated risk; the younger son may leave for a time, but in freedom he may also wake up to himself and come home.

A RIOTOUS TIME

Soon after, the younger son left for a "foreign land" where he spent his inheritance on "[*insert adjective*] living." Different

English translations choose different words to describe the kind of living the younger son does. The NIV goes with "wild" living, the CEB "extravagant" living, and I'm personally fond of the KJV's choice of "riotous" living. Like the son's demand, this is an interesting way to describe something. Later in the story, the older brother will accuse the younger of spending his money on prostitutes (Luke 15:30), but Jesus doesn't say that. Jesus says wild, extravagant, or riotous living. If Jesus had wanted to say sexually immoral, he could have. Or if he'd wanted to say "sinful" he could have. But instead, he chose a word with a bit of nuance. I have a good friend who, after his mother died, used his inheritance to get a pricey apartment and a motorcycle. Sounds like it was a wild time, for a while, but he burned through his inheritance, broke his back on the motorcycle, and then joined the army because he was out of money. That's riotous living.

Like my friend, the son burned through his inheritance, and when he'd spent it all, Jesus says, "A severe food shortage arose in that country, and he began to be in need" (verse 14). I love this strange little addition to the story. The son has made some reckless and irresponsible decisions, he's wounded his father and brother, spent his money, but now he's experiencing a difficulty outside of his control. Real life is like this. We make decisions that hurt us and others and at the same time experience hurt from outside of ourselves, and neither justifies the other.

When he ran out of money and experienced the toll of famine, Jesus says, the son took a job feeding pigs. Like all the other pieces in this story, this is a complicated one. Pigs were considered unclean by religious Jews, but owning them or feeding them wasn't technically wrong. Rabbis debate whether a Jew could engage in business that included pigs, but it's a grey issue. What is clear however, is that feeding pigs and eventually becoming so hungry that the son wants to eat what the pigs were eating is not ideal. Like my friend joining the army after he ran out of money, it's the desperate kind of move you make when you don't know what else to do. Jesus even adds a little more nuance in the story to demonstrate the difficulty of the human experience, saying, "He longed to eat his fill from what the pigs ate, but no one gave him anything" (verse 16). Not only did he experience the pain of a food shortage, now he's experiencing the failing of human generosity.

MISSING THE MARK

I want to pause here for a moment and ask you a question: How does Jesus understand sin? Sin is one of those tricky, loaded, and complicated biblical words that gets thrown around a lot. And if you're like me, it's a word that can make you tense up a bit, because you've experienced the way "sin" can be wielded like a cudgel to judge, shame, or coerce. And yet, sin is a pretty important concept in the Bible, especially in regard to the gospel. In 1 Corinthians 15:1 and 3, the apostle Paul says, "Brothers and sisters, I want to call your attention to the good news [gospel] that I preached to you. . . . Christ died for our sins in line with the scriptures." It's right there. The gospel includes Christ's death for sins. But what is sin? And how does Jesus understand sin? The reason I bring this up here is because I think we learn a lot about Jesus' understanding of sin in the parable of the prodigal son.

As we've already mentioned, our understanding of the gospel, and by extension sin, can be transactional. Within this understanding, sin is seen as an infraction or a violation of the law that accrues penalties. Sort of like getting a speeding ticket. Speeding is the sin, the citation the penalty. There's some truth to this idea, but things get a bit tricky when we read the parable of the prodigal son, because the son's actions do not technically violate the law.

The biblical word we translate as *sin* means "to miss the mark." In a transactional or legal gospel, the mark is the law. We miss the mark when we fail to live up to the standards set within the law (i.e., speeding is missing the mark of the speed limit). But again, that definition doesn't help us much with the prodigal son because he didn't miss the mark of the law. Yet we can all sense that he did miss a different mark. Something else, something deeper.

When Jesus distilled all the law into loving God, loving self, and loving others, he was helping us adjust our sights to aim at the proper target, which was and is love. Love is the aim, the target, the standard. Which means sin is not about violating a law but instead about violating love. The youngest son doesn't break the law, but he does break communion with his family, he wounds his father and brother, he isolates, and he puts himself in positions that can harm himself. Instead of seeing sin as violations of the law, Jesus shows us that sin is turning away from love, communion, and relationality. We were made to live in loving union with God, self, and others, experiencing the mutuality of good relationality. Sin is the disruption of union, mutuality, and goodness. It's what happens when we or others *turn away* from relationship. Or when we build systems of segregation and degradation that turn others away, like when no one provides a meal for the younger son. Exclusion and isolation are wrong, not simply because they violate a law, but because they cause harm.

OF JUDGMENT AND PIGS

This leads us to a second question: what is the judgment for sin? We've spent a lot of time in this chapter trying to unravel legal and transactional understandings of the gospel. But arguably the thorniest and stickiest issue regarding sin and gospel is the idea of judgment, i.e., what does God do about sin? In a transactional and legal gospel, God must judge sin. We envision God as a judge who reviews the records of our lives and, according to the law, dispenses mandatory sentences. This framing presents judgment as an active work. Meaning that God actively chooses to judge and dispense judgment. Active judgment is like grounding a child. A parent chooses to enact judgment. But in Jesus' story, there is no active judgment. The father does not banish his son, or force him into his room, nor does he use violence to coerce him into compliance. Does that mean there's no judgment?

There is judgment all throughout the parable of the prodigal son, but it always looks, feels, sounds, and tastes like other-oriented love. This plays out in two ways. First, the younger son experiences judgment in the natural consequences of his actions. He demands his inheritance, spends it on riotous living, and comes to the end of his rope. Those are the natural consequences of sin. If I repeatedly lie to my wife so much that she stops trusting me, I am experiencing the judgment of natural consequences. God is not actively punishing me; I am experiencing the real-world cost of being deceptive, of missing the mark of love.

God consents to our decisions and allows us to pursue our own ends. We'll call that "intrinsic judgment" vs. active judgment because our actions and decisions have intrinsic consequences. This is how the apostle Paul describes judgment in his letter to the Romans. Three different times, Paul says, "God gave them over" (NIV) to their desires, their actions, and their consequences (Romans 1:24, 26, 28). Like the younger son, God grants our request and gives us the freedom to choose what we want.

However, consent is only one part of the story, because God consents and at the same time never gives up. Theologian Brad Jersak says, "Beyond gravity there is also grace."[2] Yes, we often experience the consequence of our sin, but God never gives up on us. God is always searching for us, sending partners to comfort, and, like the father in the prodigal son parable, scanning the horizon for any sign of a lost child. God grants our request, a calculated risk in love, but then he, in Jesus, packs his bags and heads out with us.

That leads us to the second kind of judgment in the parable—grace. Grace is a kind of judgment we rarely understand, and often minimize. When the younger son demands his inheritance, the father grants it. Whatever story or lie the younger son had told himself to justify this painful action has been revealed and that's a gift, but it's also hard. And when the younger son experiences the intrinsic judgment of his actions and decides to come home, he is met by his father, who restores him as a son. And that too is a gift but a painful kind of reveal, because it confronts the son with the truth of his wound, his recklessness, and most importantly, his belovedness. It's easy to write that kind of judgment off, but being confronted by love is a startling affront to everything that made us run away in the first place. This is why, after telling us that God "gives us over" to our sin, Paul goes on to say, it is the kindness of God that leads to a change of heart (Romans 2:4). God consents but never gives up. He always chases us to offer us kindness and a way home.

THE PLAN

In the fields, with the pigs, the son "came to his senses" (Luke 15:17). Something in him wakes up and he remembers his father's home, the food, and the way even servants had more than enough to eat. So he concocts a plan: "I will get up and go to my father, and say to him, 'Father, I have sinned against heaven and against you. I no longer deserve to be called your son. Take me on as one of your hired hands'" (verses 18–19). The son's plan is simple—he'll ask for a job. He'll return to his father, not as a son but as an employee. The son recognizes that he no longer deserves to be called a son but maybe, just maybe, he can earn his way into good standing with his father. Maybe if he works hard enough and proves that he's changed, he can live in the house again.

Biblical scholars debate if the phrase "came to his senses" is meant to imply genuine heart change or simply the realization that life was better at his father's home. I lean towards the second option because the son's plan misses the most important issues. His mindset is transactional; he thinks that if he can work hard enough, he'll earn forgiveness. But that's not how repair works. Giving my dad twenty bucks after I shouted, "You're not my real dad," would have done nothing to repair the wound I may have caused. If anything, it's offensive. I think if I had tried to do that my dad would have laughed and said something like, "Where did you get that money in the first place?" Which is a fair question: how could I possibly pay my dad back with his own money? It's silly. Yet that is so often how our gospel works. We transform God into a debt collector who is obsessed with the ledger. Debts must be paid back. Outstanding fees must be settled.

But look what happens in Jesus' story. When the son approaches his father's house, Jesus tells us,

While he was still a long way off, his father saw him and was moved with compassion. His father ran to him, hugged him, and kissed him. Then his son said, "Father, I have sinned against heaven and against you. I no longer deserve to be called your son." But the father said to his servants, "Quickly, bring out the best robe and put it on him! Put a ring on his finger and sandals on his feet! Fetch the fattened calf and slaughter it. We must celebrate with feasting because this son of mine was dead and has come back to life! He was lost and is found!" And they began to celebrate. (verses 20–24)

Before the son can even negotiate terms, the father shushes him, clothes him with finery, and gets the barbecue going. There's not one word about wasted inheritance, debts, penalties, or guilt. The father doesn't seem to care. All he cares about is his son. Money doesn't bring dead things to life, or lost things home.

JANE'S CAR

A couple years ago, a friend of mine, whom we'll call Jane, was living through a particularly trying time. *Trying* is an understatement; it was more like an earth-shattering, mind-bending, heartbreaking kind of time. I won't tell you the details, that's Jane's story to tell. What I want to tell you about is one particular episode in that particular season of Jane's life. While everything else was going on, Jane's car broke down and had to be taken to a mechanic, and a co-worker of Jane's offered to lend her her own car in the interim. That's a generous offer, but Jane is one of the most responsible people I know—if I was going to lend my car to anyone, it would be her. She's the kind of person who would return your car cleaner than it was before. The kind of person who could fill the car with gas and get you an oil change. The kind of person who would organize your center console and magically return your car with less miles on it. You get it. Except, that is not what happened. Instead, Jane was in an accident that resulted in her friend's car being totaled.

When Jane told me this story, I could feel every muscle in my body tense until it felt like I had been in the accident. I think if this had happened to me, I'd be tempted to just disappear. To leave the totaled car in the street and walk directly into the ocean. Bye friends. Bye life. If you'd like to reach me, send a message to P.O. Box *Jonny does not exist anymore*. But Jane is made of steel, so she called her friend to tell her what had happened. And the most amazing thing occurred. Her friend asked her if she was okay. She told Jane not to worry about the car, they'd cover it. They just wanted to know if she was okay. Jane told me she didn't even know what to do with that kind of thing. It was a kind of grace and generosity that made her uncomfortable. And to be honest, it makes me uncomfortable too. It makes me uncomfortable in the same way the gospel does.

The father's response to the younger son is like that. The younger son took the keys to the car and drove it right off the cliff. In the aftermath his mind swirls with numbers, calculations, and ledgers. He wonders if he can pay his father back. Work his way into good standing. But when the father sees his son, he says, "I don't care about the car! I care about you." In the same way, God does not need to be paid back. Instead, the debt is absorbed and canceled. This is what the apostle Paul says, writing in Colossians: "[God] destroyed the record of the debt we owed, with its requirements that worked against us. He canceled it by nailing it to the cross" (Colossians 2:14).

In the last chapter we introduced the idea of Jubilee and restoration. What happened to Jane was Jubilee. What happened to the younger son when he returned home was Jubilee. God does not hold debt over our heads and demand repayment, God cancels debt and destroys the record. God can do this, because God is big enough to absorb the loss and so loving that he doesn't even blink an eye at it. It's not that God doesn't care about the car, but God owns all cars and is more concerned about you and me and whomever else might have been harmed in the accident. Jubilee is about canceling debt and restoring life to wholeness. When Jane's friend said, "We'll take care of the car," she was offering Jane a Jubilee kind of love. Absorbing the loss so that Jane could find her way back to wholeness. In the same way, when the father shushes the son and clothes him, he is absorbing the loss and offering his son a chance at wholeness.

STORIES WE TELL

I want to rewind a bit here. Before the son makes it to his father's home, he plans to tell his father, "I no longer deserve to be called your son. Take me on as one of your hired hands" (verse 19). Do you think the son believes that? I think he does, because I've been there. When I told my dad, "You're not my real dad," it had almost nothing to do with him and everything to do with me. The nineties were a particularly angsty time— we youths hated everything from math, to parents, to belts. But I also felt alone. I was the only kid I knew, at the time, who'd lost a parent and been left behind by his brothers (more on that later), and that kind of solitary grief can make you feel like an alien on your own planet. Shouting and jabbing at my stepdad was my way of sending out probes to confirm that the air really *was* as hostile as I imagined it was. *Better stay in the ship, the landscape is toxic.*

I had bought into a story that I was alone, a little green man far from home. Stories like that have a way of shaping you. I'd go to parties, and either be the center of attention or the emo kid sitting on the front lawn, smoking a cigarette and searching the sky for my home planet while I wondered if anyone noticed that I had left. Even today, all these years later, my triggers are still isolation, invisibility, and loneliness. Which is kind of wild because I'm hard to forget. I'm loud, I have a huge face, and I am, objectively, the funniest (my wife would add most obnoxious) person you know. I've learned to be these things to cope with feeling invisible. So that you, my brothers, my dead dad, or God would never forget me again.

I wonder if that's why the youngest son said what he did. I wonder if he ever believed he deserved to be a son. If demanding his inheritance was a test, a probe to measure the love of his father. I wonder if that's why he left. If he felt uncomfortable with the answers.

When the son demanded his inheritance, the father gave it to him. When the son left, the father let him go. We've already called that *love*, but it's a kind of love that makes me uncomfortable. It's the kind of love that does not coerce, control, or make ultimatums. It's the kind of love that sits with us at the dining room table after we've just shouted, "You're not my real dad," until we grow comfortable with a love that does not meet us in kind, but in kindness. When my dad sat quietly with me, he met me with a kind of love that refused to confirm my story. He was present when presence is what I questioned. I sent out a probe that read "home," but that scared me. It still kind of does.

When the son returns, rehearsing his story—"I do not deserve to be called your son, but I can work for it if you let me"—he doesn't know what will happen. This is another probe, another test to determine what remains after he pressed self-destruct and jettisoned himself into another land. Again, here's what Jesus says:

> While he was still a long way off, his father saw him and was moved with compassion. His father ran to him, hugged him, and kissed him. Then his son said, "Father, I have sinned against heaven and against you. I no longer deserve to be called your son." But the father said to his servants, "Quickly, bring out the best robe and put it on him! Put a ring on his finger and sandals on his feet! Fetch the fattened calf and slaughter it. We must celebrate with feasting because this son of mine was dead and has come back to life! He was lost and is found!" And they began to celebrate. (verses 20–24)

Before the son can finish his sentence, the father clothes him in the garments of sonship. That's what the robe and ring imply. Without work, or effort, or even transactional negotiations, the son is back in. Like my dad, the father meets the son with a disquieting kind of love. The son is counting the cost, measuring the loss, but the father is telling his son, "You can't pay me back, I won't even let you try."

You can't earn sonship. You can't cover wounds in money. You can't pay for resurrection. Those are all gifts. All we can do is receive them, or not. That's what makes this love disquieting and uncomfortable—we could even call it a judgment. If we could earn our place in the family, then we'd have some measure of control. But control is what got us here. Sure, it was a riotous time, but my back is breaking from the weight of a story that does not serve me well, and unlike my friend, I just don't think I could join the army, though I do like pigs. The question is simply, do I receive the gift? Will the younger son receive the gift of restoration? Will he see himself as the father clearly already does—a son? Or will he try, by the weight of his own bootstraps, to earn a thing that was always already his?

QUESTIONS

1. Talking about our relationship with God is probably not new for you, but the ways we have discussed it in this chapter might have provided a new or different way of talking about ideas like sin and judgment. Does placing ideas like sin within the context of relationship and love expand or challenge your previous thinking? If so, in what ways?

2. Why do you think Jesus tells such a convoluted story? Do you think there is a reason why Jesus doesn't use more black and white examples to make his point?

3. Do you think the younger son came home because of genuine heart change or because of a desperate situation? Do you think the answer matters to God?

4. At this point in the story, how does the father compare or contrast to your images of God?

Prayer
God, help me trust you. I hear that you love me and that you always welcome me home but my upbringing, my tradition, my experience often testifies to transactions. Sometimes it feels

easier to be a hired servant than a son or daughter because trust is a gamble that has cost me too much to make again. So, God, would you sit with me and walk with me? Would you be present when I question presence? Would you meet me on the road and quiet my anxious stories? Would you meet me in kindness not in kind, so that I might know what you've always said is true?

Amen.

THREE

Prodigal Son, Part 2

Now his older son was in the field. Coming in from the field, he approached the house and heard music and dancing. He called one of the servants and asked what was going on. The servant replied, "Your brother has arrived, and your father has slaughtered the fattened calf because he received his son back safe and sound." Then the older son was furious and didn't want to enter in, but his father came out and begged him. He answered his father, "Look, I've served you all these years, and I never disobeyed your instruction. Yet you've never given me as much as a young goat so I could celebrate with my friends. But when this son of yours returned, after gobbling up your estate on prostitutes, you slaughtered the fattened calf for him." Then his father said, "Son, you are always with me, and everything I have is yours. But we had to celebrate and be glad because this brother of yours was dead and is alive. He was lost and is found." (Luke 15:25–32)

My final month of writing this book was a hectic one. It was the last month of summer, and my wife Tory and I had a full schedule. The first of the month we did a thirty-mile river trip with some of our closest friends. Then Tory put on a weekend-long summer camp for thirty of our friends, which required me to spend more time at Costco than I feel comfortable telling you. After that, the church where I worked hosted our end of summer, beginning of fall party. When we weren't floating, camping, working, or planning, I tried to write.

The month started well. We were in good spirits and excited for a full of month of beautiful events. We got through the first half of the month feeling rosy, but by the end of the month my positive outlook was beginning to wear thin. I started feeling anxiety about work and the book deadline and became a little testy. Tory would ask for something and I'd snap back. If I felt like I'd been away from writing too long, I'd get tense and abrasive. I can be a little sensitive when I'm stressed.

By the end of the month, we had made it through, and our final week was supposed to be smooth sailing. We had nothing planned, work was normal, and my free time was dedicated to finishing up this book. That was all true in theory, but emotionally I was in a different place. My characteristically optimistic persona was gone, and I was clean out of patience, grace, or self-awareness. It all came to a head Tuesday morning.

I had a meeting at ten a.m. but needed to load up my truck with a few things from summer camp. As I was getting ready to leave, I asked Tory if she would help me load a fire pit into the back of the truck and she, like a normal person, said, "Yeah, just give me a minute to put some shoes on." That's what she said, but something stupid happened in my brain and what I heard was, "Calm down, your time's not that important, I'll be there when I'm good and ready." I repeat, that is not what she said. I don't even think she had a weird tone. But my brain went haywire. I didn't immediately snap back; instead—like the grown-up I am—I stewed on it until we'd gotten the fire pit in the back of the truck, and then with minutes to get to my meeting, I unloaded on her. I told her how I felt like I'd worked *so hard* on all her projects but couldn't get her to prioritize mine. I said things like, "my life and my stuff play second string to yours." And stuff like, "I sacrifice for you but can't get you to help me get a G*$ D@%^ firepit from *your* event in the back of the truck, which I'm doing for you!" It was a lot, and it was wrong.

I could immediately see the hurt on Tory's face. Those were brutal things to say to someone who loves me well and has sacrificed so much for me. Somehow, despite my cruelty, Tory was kind and truthful. She reminded me that I'd eagerly made those commitments. I wasn't a victim in this story, I had chosen to participate. She then helped me see, as she's done before, that this is a bit of a pattern for me. I overcommit, say yes to everything, sacrifice my own time with a smile, but then start to feel like I'm forgotten despite how many times she checks in with me. And it's true, I do that. I can jump between hero and victim pretty quickly. One moment I can do anything and everything; write a book, cook for thirty people, co-lead a church, be a good friend, be an even better husband, go to the gym, pay the bills, fix a leak, pray, fish, read nerdy articles, and say yes to every speaking invitation. I try to hold it all together and sometimes I can, at least for a while. But eventually my knees buckle under the weight of my artificially inflated superhero cape, so I take it off and don my alter ego of victim.

When I'm dressed as a victim, everyone and everything becomes a threat. That's always the first sign. I start to blame people for not working hard enough. They don't carry their weight like I do. I'm out here doing the hard work while they're over there, enjoying the fruit of my labor. I've sacrificed while they have played. Then I start to feel forgotten, like everyone is inside the party while I'm out here alone, cleaning up the empty bottles. If that's all left to fester too long, things get dark. I'll blame and hide. I'll villainize and bite. I'll unleash a torrent of a painful lies on my wife on a sunny Tuesday morning.

I can be a real older brother sometimes. Thankfully, my wife is a lot like the father and knows how to welcome me home.

OLDER BROTHERS

I can never quite decide which brother I am more like. Most of the time I feel like a younger brother, and yet I can be a real older brother. I am a religious leader and "insider" with years of academic training. I've worked hard and made religiously right choices. And as the story above illustrates, I can dance between hero and victim with the best of them. I can also be judgy, temperamental, and slow to celebrate the homecoming of my perceived younger brothers. The genius of Jesus' storytelling is that it provides us the room to see ourselves in every character. We can be the lost younger brother, the obstinate older brother, and even the gracious father—sometimes within the span of a few seconds.

Whichever brother you identify with most, it's easy to treat the older brother like a supporting actor, a minor player in the younger's story, included less to further the narrative and more to shade the Pharisees and religious experts. But I don't think that's what Jesus intended. If Jesus had merely wanted to criticize the Pharisees and legal experts, he could have ended the parable with the younger's return as he'd done in previous stories about the lost coin and lost sheep (Luke 15:1–10). Why waste time talking about an obstinate partygoer when you can just describe the party they're not at? Yet that's not what Jesus does. Jesus includes the Pharisees and legal experts, giving them their own act, nearly as long as the first, in which they take center stage alongside the father.

Jesus is telling us something important here: this is as much the older brother's story as it is the younger's. The older brother is not an addendum or a subplot, but an essential participant in the good news Jesus is sharing. As the apostle Paul wrote in Ephesians 2:17, "When he [Jesus] came, he announced the good news of peace to you who were far away from God and to those who were near." This is a story for brothers near and far. For the ones who fled *and* the ones who stayed. Everyone is invited to the table.

That's good news, the best news even, but it's a hard truth, because older brothers are hard to love, especially when you are one. In the parable, older brothers represent the religious leaders who are the most ardent critics of Jesus. When Jesus heals a man on the Sabbath (John 5), the Pharisees become incensed. Who cares, you may be thinking, a man was healed, so shouldn't we celebrate? But the Pharisees do care, and they don't seem all that interested in celebrating. When the disciples pick stalks of wheat to eat while walking through a field (Mark 2:23–24), the Pharisees accuse Jesus of violating religious law. How can that possibly matter? It was a snack. But not for the Pharisees. They care a lot about what people eat and drink and when, and it's not because they're counting macros. At every turn, the Pharisees seek to hinder Jesus' work, eventually condemning him to death, and it's challenging to feel much empathy for that.

And yet, just as hard as it is to love an older brother, it's hard to receive love when you're an older brother. This is especially true for the Pharisees and religious experts who have spent a lifetime working hard on what they believed was Israel's behalf. By the time of Jesus, Israel had been conquered by a veritable who's who of empires and the Pharisees believed their peoples' subjugation was due to their unfaithfulness to God. They hoped, prayed, and worked hard to lead Israel back into good standing with God for theirs and their kinsmen's liberation. That is why, when the religious leaders and Pharisees see Jesus with tax collectors and sinners, they get angry—they worry their hard work will be undone and Israel will suffer even more. They've taken on the responsibility of saving Israel and Jesus is a threat to them and their efforts. I don't agree with the Pharisees and religious experts, but as a man learning to put away his cape, I do have empathy for them.

Jesus' invitation is a challenge for older brothers because it cuts to the core of their—honestly, my—identity. Jesus invites everyone to the table, to sit side by side without class or category, freed to be our truest selves. That's good news if you're a younger brother with little to lose, but a difficult thing to accept if you're an older brother who has spent a lifetime proving your value and inflating your cape. This is why Jesus says it's impossible for the rich to enter the kingdom of heaven—some of us have a lot to lose.

REFUSING A PARTY

We first meet the older brother during the younger's party. The older brother has been out dutifully working his father's fields, and as he returns home, he "heard music and dancing" (Luke 15:25). What does he do? He stops. Which is fascinating. Who hears music and dancing coming from their own home and stops? Who refuses to go to a party THEY are hosting? (All the introverts are like, "Me. I stop.")

Instead of entering the party himself, the older brother called a servant and "asked what was going on" (verse 26). The servant replied, "Your brother has arrived, and your father has slaughtered the fattened calf because he received his son back safe and sound" (verse 27). When the older brother heard the news, he became "furious and didn't want to enter in" (verse 28). What a response. His lost younger brother has finally returned and instead of feeling joy or relief, he feels anger.

It can be easy to villainize the older brother. But we need to pause and consider his plight. The older brother has suffered at the hand of the younger. The younger cursed his father and by extension the older brother. The younger demanded his inheritance, a portion of the family's livelihood, which the father gave, and then he spent it in irredeemable ways. Meaning, it won't come back. Can't be returned. And yes, that was the father's estate, but it was also the older brother's. He'd worked those fields, poured his heart and blood into the land, and someday it would have been his. But now there's less. And even if they could rebuild what the younger had destroyed, there's the emotional wound to tend to. The younger abandoned the family. He left the older brother to work the fields alone. To grow up alone.

The older brother has suffered, he harbors a real wound. And when we see it that way, it makes perfect sense why he wouldn't celebrate the younger's return. When he hears about the younger and sees the party, his loss resurfaces, sending fearful signals throughout his body. His brain goes liminal, and he freezes outside the party unable to enter, afraid of a returning threat, an approaching predator.

FEAR AND LOATHING

Fear is a strange thing, especially when left to simmer. Untended, fear grows; it doesn't dissipate, it seethes and metastasizes. It works its way into our bodies, our minds, and eventually our imaginations, until all the world feels fearful. What started as a real wound becomes our vision of the world. We become hyperaware of loss and lack, constantly avoiding, and fighting potential threats. Brené Brown calls this "scarcity."[1]

Both brothers experience scarcity in their own way. The younger demands his inheritance and leaves. There's too little time, money, and love, so he'll take what's his and leave. But in older brothers, scarcity engenders a different response. We don't bail, we manage. We work. We go to the fields and labor away, heaping on ourselves greater and greater levels of responsibility. This is easy to see in religious circles, because religion provides a streamlined way to manage our fear: read your Bible, go to church, tithe, don't sin, don't have sex before marriage, and on and on—in a word, obey.

We can bring the same energy to our jobs, our relationships, or any other part of our lives we're afraid of losing. The problem is it doesn't work. Scarcity is fueled, not fulfilled, by hard work. This is true whether we succeed or fail at managing our fear. If I fail, I just go back and try harder. *Maybe if I really try, I can make it work.* Instead of revealing the wound, failure can convince us of the lie that we just need to try harder, be better, work more. But success is just as problematic, because the weight never gets lifted. Success doesn't satiate fear, it raises the stakes and moves the goalposts. Meaning we need to work even harder to maintain our sense of control.

DARK LOGIC

Fear and scarcity are so difficult to disrupt because they are located in real loss. In older brothers, fear hides behind good logic. Allowing the younger brother to come home isn't smart. He's a threat, a thief, a vagabond. How do we know he won't steal again? And the truth is, we don't. The older brother isn't wrong. That's what makes fear so tricky—it's rooted in a kind of truth. It may not be the whole truth, or the only truth, but it is a truth the older brother experienced and to compromise on that truth feels wrong.

Look at what happens when the father comes to entreat the older brother. The older brother defends himself by making two profound accusations. The first accusation is against the younger brother: "This son of yours returned, after gobbling up your estate on prostitutes" (verse 30). The accusation is partly, but not wholly, true. The younger son did gobble up the inheritance, but we don't know what he spent it on. Jesus only says "extravagant living"—it's the older brother who colors in the details by adding "on prostitutes." That's a rewrite, an addition, an assumption, a judgment without evidence or context. The older brother assumes the worst of the younger—he's not just a thief, he's a philanderer. The older brother doesn't know what happened, so he fills in the gaps with worst-case scenarios and dark deeds. This is what fear and scarcity do. They make us assume the worst. We hear the music and dancing and instead of seeing a party, see a plot. A ploy to take more and leave less.

It's a dangerous logic, because as soon as we convince ourselves of the worst, we can justify the worst in ourselves.

Exclusion, gatekeeping, and even violence become justifiable means of protecting ourselves, our estates, our communities, our culture, our *fill in the gap*. And it feels right! Of course it does—he's not a younger brother, he's a destroyer of worlds, here to do again what he did before. The older brother *must* protect himself and his father. This is the most insidious and profound defense the older brother makes. Remember what he said to the father, "after gobbling up *your estate*" (emphasis added). The older brother uses the father's loss as justification for his actions. The older brother manipulates the truth for his own purposes. The father did suffer, the father was cursed and abandoned. But nowhere in the story does the father name these grievances. No, this is the dark logic of fear and scarcity. It blames, hides, and justifies.

The second accusation is interesting: it's not aimed at the younger brother, but at the father. Here is what the older brother said, with italics added for emphasis: "When this *son of yours* returned, after gobbling up *your* estate on prostitutes, *you* slaughtered the fattened calf for him" (verse 30). It's like the older brother is blaming the father for the younger's action, the loss of inheritance, and the celebration. You raised him this way, you let him go, and now you are celebrating with him. This is as much on you as it is on him, and I won't be complicit in your bad parenting. I won't just sit idly by and watch him steal from us again.

The older brother is right, at least partially. The father did let the younger go and he is celebrating his return. To the older brother, the father is complicit. He could have prevented this, but he didn't. And I think that's also one of the reasons the older brother refuses to enter the party. He's afraid it would make him complicit too. That if he enters the party, he is tacitly endorsing or overlooking the younger brother's actions. And he can't. It's not just pride or fear, either—if you've experienced trauma, then you know that silence about pain can cause more pain. The injury compounds in silence, fracturing under the weight of quiet complicity—even, or maybe especially, when it's our own silence about our own pain.

RESENTMENT AND RESTITUTION

Scarcity is not immune to love. We can love someone and believe the worst about them. We can love someone and at the very same time believe they are a threat. In fact, that's normally the case. We often fear the people we love the most because they're the ones who can hurt and have hurt us the most. It's easy to assume the older brother does not love the younger, but I don't think that's true. He is his younger brother after all. As a kid who spent a long time waiting for the return of his brother (we'll get to that story later), I believe the older loved the younger and longed for his return. Why won't he celebrate then? Because he wants to see some restitution.

In fear and scarcity, older brothers impose on themselves impossible weights. We work hard, plow the fields, and pay the cost to stay. The more we pay, the harder we work, the more our scarcity and fear metastasize into resentment. The older brother resents his younger for abandoning him in the fields. But he also resents the father for allowing the younger brother to leave and then celebrating his return. The older brother feels like he's been treated unfairly. Like he's paid while everyone else has played. This is what he says to the father: "Look, I've served you all these years, and I never disobeyed your instruction. Yet you've never given me as much as a young goat so I could celebrate with my friends" (verse 29). He is in effect saying, where's my party? I stayed, I worked, I obeyed. I did all the right things and yet you never rewarded me.

Resentment is the bitterness we feel at being treated unfairly. We did our part and are now resentful because we don't see everyone else doing theirs. The father keeps giving, the son keeps taking, but when will they stop and come to the fields and work a little? I think the older would accept the younger's return *if* he just worked a little first. Scarcity is not immune to love; it just wants to see some effort. Some restitution, some recompense, some pain.

The German philosopher Friedrich Nietzsche (you didn't see that coming, did you), believed equality was a value rooted in envy—envy of the other who has what we want and enjoys it. Therefore, justice is the demand that the enjoyment of the other should be stopped.[2] I don't believe Nietzsche was right— he was a very depressed German who didn't get invited to a lot of parties—but I think he was naming the dark logic of older brothers. We hide our loss, our wounds, our pain behind a smoke screen of justice, equity, protection, and good logic. We wield the pain of our father to justify our actions, all the while hiding the fact that we hurt too. That we want to be rewarded, that we want a party.

We older brothers want the younger to return, I think we genuinely do, but we want to know he's worked for it. That it cost him as much as it's cost us. That he's suffered as much as we have. That he's paid, that he's felt the pain, that he knows the weight we carry, that he knows the loss we endured. That he knows how hard it was for us. That we're not alone, not abandoned, that our work wasn't in vain. That after all these years of toiling in his absence, he woke up to our suffering.

That's the secret. We want our pain to be seen and if we don't carefully and compassionately tend to it, it will assert itself. It will explode in violent, manipulative displays. Claiming justice, but demanding retribution.

IMPOSING JUDGMENT

We hide our fear and anger behind good things like equity and justice. The older brother justifies his rage and pain, using the father's wound, but here's the thing—the father doesn't. At no point in the entire story does the father demand judgment, repayment, or retribution. He's suffered, most directly, at the hand of the younger son but does not once name his own grievance. Why is that? Because the father is uninterested in retribution. He wants reunion.

Here is a hard truth we, younger and older siblings alike, must wrestle with. We are far more obsessed with judgment than our father is. The younger brother returns, rehearsing a shame narrative and expecting to be judged by the father, while the older seethes in the field demanding judgment and retribution. But that's not what the father does; he doesn't shame, judge, or demand. No, shame and judgment are imposed by the sons onto themselves and each other. It emerges from their own dark stories and twisted fantasies and is then projected onto the father.

How much of our own theology, our thoughts about God, are like that? Projections of our fear more than images of truth? Is God a wrathful judge, or are we? Does God impose new and heavier laws, or do we? Does God demand retribution and judgment, or do we? The famous psychoanalyst, Sigmund Freud (another turn!), believed the weights of shame and judgment we feel come mostly from within and not outside ourselves, stemming from what he called the *superego*. The superego is the self-critical part of our conscious that is formed throughout our lives. It comes from experiences we have with parents, friends, teachers, and religious traditions. It's the part of our psyche shaped by fear, loss, and scarcity that now whispers to us stories of condemnation, shame, and threat.

The apostle Paul had his own version of the superego, what he called "the law of sin and death." In Paul's mind, there are multiple laws at work within us. One is the "law of the Spirit of life" while the other is the "law of sin and death" (Romans 8:2). These two laws wage war in our bodies—as Paul says, "I see a different law at work in my body. It wages a war against the law of my mind and takes me prisoner with the law of sin that is in my body" (Romans 7:23). Paul is describing an impulse, an instinct, a whispering superego that lives in our bodies. That doesn't mean our bodies are bad, please don't hear that. It means we've learned and habituated this law in ways that bypass our rational faculties. Like the superego, it's deep inside us and acts on muscle memory.

But here is the crucial thing to understand: "the law of sin and death" does not come from God. It comes from within us and then projects onto God false images. Our loss, our fear, our scarcity, our resentment are superimposed onto God, transforming God into the worst parts of ourselves. And just as we justify our fear behind words like justice and equity, we justify our version of God with words like holiness and righteousness. We read the story through our dark logic, filling in the gaps with our painful gospel. We teach it in church, Sunday school, and seminary. We hand it down from one generation to the next, concretizing our fear-addled idols in the imagination of younger minds, saying, "This is what God is like!" When the truth is, this is what we are like.

THE FATHER'S RESPONSE

The older brother is angry and afraid, frozen outside the party and unable to enter. What happens next is my favorite part of the entire story, because as the father is celebrating, dancing, and delighting in the return of his son, he notices something. He looks around, sees friends, neighbors, and extended family but realizes his eldest son is missing. What does the father do? He leaves the party to search for his son.

Can we pause right there for a moment? Every time I read this part of the story I'm shook. This is *the* moment the father has been waiting who knows how long for. His son is finally home, the barbecue is lit, the dancing has started. If I'm the father, there's no way I'm leaving the party. It would be like leaving my wedding to chase a grumpy groomsman. I'm not doing it, this is my day, you get in line or get out! But that's not what the father does. He leaves his party to find his boy.

Jesus began this parable by telling two others. In the first, a shepherd loses one of his one hundred sheep. When he realizes what's happened, he leaves the ninety-nine behind and goes searching for the one. When he finds the missing sheep, he throws a party and invites everyone to join. In the second, a woman loses one of her ten coins and when she realizes it, tears apart her home to find the missing coin. And again, when she finally does, she calls up her friends and celebrates. Each image emphasizes the value of the lost thing and the desperate measures taken to find them. The parable of the prodigal sons is following a similar pattern; if you were listening, you'd expect the *lost, found, celebration* equation to continue. Yet Jesus does something unexpected. He adds a twist, a turn in the tale, a misdirect. Because who could have imagined there was another lost boy in this story, hiding just outside in the fields alone?

And who could have predicted the father would leave his party in search of this, his valuable and beloved eldest son?

Tell me that's not good news.

POETIC IRONY

The father leaves the party and searches for his son. We don't know how long it takes, Jesus doesn't include that detail—it's a gap for us to fill with our own stories. But eventually he locates his eldest son. I wonder if it's a spot the eldest has hidden in before. Maybe the place he'd go when he was afraid. Or the place he hid after his brother left. Somewhere safe in the fields, where only his father could find him. Maybe a place he knew his father would come looking.

When the father finds his son, he begs him to come into the party. But quickly the conversation turns, and the older brother, full of pent-up energy, explodes, like a pressure cooker, onto the father. In a rush, he unleashes all his fury; he blames and hides, accuses, and victimizes; he lets it all out. And the father listens. The father patiently endures the tirade and absorbs the fear. He doesn't judge, he doesn't condemn, he doesn't shame, he doesn't demand, and he doesn't silence. He listens and creates space for the older brother to expose the lie and reveal the wound at the bottom of everything. And when the older brother has exhausted himself and stands there, breathless, waiting for either vindication or condemnation, the father says the most disarming and beautiful of things: "Son, you are always with me, and everything I have is yours" (verse 31).

The poetic irony of older brothers is that the very things we're afraid of losing—the things we fight to protect, the things we want the most—are already ours. The older brother wanted a party, to which the father responds, "Why didn't you throw one?" The older brother is angry he has never come in from the fields to a meal, to which the father responds, "I've had the table set this whole time, I've been waiting for you, just inside."

"Everything I have is already yours."

In fear and scarcity, we miss the truth that the very things we want are already ours. Instead of receiving our gift and celebrating, we stay in the field working. We keep checking the ledger to make sure everyone has paid their fair share. We keep our nose to the grindstone to make sure we don't fall behind. We guard the door from threats and predators to make sure no one steals again. But at the end of the day, who does it cost the most? Us! In our need for others to pay, we keep paying. In our fear of losing, we cost ourselves the very things we're most afraid of losing. The party is right here, in our own home. All we have to do is come in from the field.

LOST BOY

This might sound strange, considering my sharp words for older brothers, but I love the story of the older brother. There is something so deeply human about him. Yes, he can be a real stick in the mud but honestly, so can I. Yeah, it's a bit weird that he cynically watches a party at his own house from the front yard, but I've done that too. Sometimes I want to run like a younger brother and other times I want to don an artificially inflated superhero cape and act like I'm better than everyone around me. And if I get really honest with myself, sometimes I feel threatened by the inclusion of others. I love the older brother because he's me on any given Tuesday morning.

But I also love the older brother because of what he represents. As we've already mentioned, the older brother represents the religious leaders of Israel. They are insiders who represent the most important cultural institution (religion) and with it wield a considerable amount of power. By including them in this story Jesus does two important things. First, he confronts them and second, he invites them in, and both with a kind of compassion I have trouble understanding.

First, Jesus confronts the way the religious authorities have excluded others. They have erected barriers to belonging and inclusion. They have held tight to their power and drawn the circle of belonging so close to themselves that not even Jesus can get in. Jesus looks at them and says, "In excluding your younger brother, you've excluded yourself."

Jesus' words remind me of the words of James Baldwin. James Baldwin's book *The Fire Next Time* takes the form of a letter written to his nephew about the Black experience in 1960s America. Baldwin writes about the kind of bodied exclusion his nephew would experience, but says something so beautifully disarming about the people who do the excluding, writing, "These men are your brothers—your lost, younger brothers. And if the word integration means anything, this is what it means: that we, with love, shall force our brothers to see themselves as they are, to cease fleeing from reality and begin to change it."[3] *The* parable of the prodigal son offers a kind of hard love to the Pharisees, religious leaders, and people like me that reveals who we really are. That's a challenging love that will feel like judgment—because it is—but it's also a liberating kind of love that invites us into the shared fellowship of our humanity.

Second, Jesus confronts the religious leaders with his invitation to belong. Jesus invites them into the party, just as the father invites the older brother. They are wanted and welcomed, like the younger brother. This can be their party too! But to

enter the party and sit beside their younger brother is to recognize that they were wrong. That they were wrong to exclude
their younger brother, wrong to blame the father, wrong to hide
away from the family, and even wrong to deny themselves the
gift of their family. Jesus' invitation to the Pharisees is genuine; he really wants them at the party. But the question now
becomes theirs to answer. Do they want to be at the party? Do
they want to sit in equity with their siblings and in fellowship
with their father?

BLESSED ARE THE BULLIES

This is where Jesus ends the parable (well, almost). We don't
know what happens next. We don't know if the older brother
receives his father's invitation or if he chooses to stay in the field.
The father will not force the older brother to come to the party;
he meets him and entreats him, but he will not coerce him. That
is not how this father works. The eldest son is free to choose.

It's a brilliant and frustrating way to end a story. In effect,
Jesus is rolling the ball into our court and asking, "What do
you want to do?" Do you want to receive what has always
been yours? Enjoy the gift, sit at the table, and reconnect with
your younger brother. Or do you want to stay out here away
from the food and the lights?

At first glance we might assume it's an easy choice. Of course
we will come inside. But to enter the party requires a kind of
death. A death to the lie, to the scapegoating, to the accusations, to the blame and threats, and to all sinister voices that
whisper laws of sin and death. To return to Freud, it requires
an ego death. A death of the false self. And yes, the false self is
the cause of so much pain and exclusion, but the false self has
also protected the wounded older brother. To tear down the

false self exposes the wound. The wound must be exposed to be healed, we need to tend to our trauma, but the truth is it feels so risky. It feels like dying, because in a way, it is.

The Episcopal priest Robert Farrar Capon calls the parable of the prodigal son a story of both grace and judgment, writing, "the classic parable of grace, therefore, turns out by anticipation to be a classic parable of judgement as well. It proclaims that grace operates only by raising the dead."[4] There is a judgment in this parable, but it doesn't operate out of fear or scarcity. It doesn't demand retribution or recompense. It's unlike the judgments either brother offers, or the ones we project onto God. The father's "judgment" is grace. It is the generous gift of more. We will explore this in greater detail later, but the way the father "judges" is to chase the older into the field, give himself, and offer the older brother the very thing he believes he's lost. And when confronted by the truth, when faced with the love of the father and the invitation to belong, the older brother must decide what to do with it. That's the judgment. It's nothing more and nothing less than the truth that you are loved and wanted at the party. It's good news, the best news in fact, but it's also hard because it requires a confrontation with ourselves.

The question is simply, what do we want? The father does not coerce or make ultimatums—this is a real choice. We get to choose what we want and honestly, either one will feel a bit like death. It will hurt to die to the false self, it will be painful to expose the wound, but hiding it will eventually destroy us. That may not sound like very good news, but I am convinced the only way to live is to die and the only way to heal is to expose the wound and tend to the fear. I believe the father's party is better than our fear and scarcity. But I can't lie to you, it's a bit risky. There's a whole world of unexplored possibilities in that party, and some of them are a bit dangerous. The father never said the party would be safe. After all, the younger brother is inside, and we don't know what he'll do next. But the promise isn't safety, the promise is a party. I think that's what faith is—it is the risk we take towards the party. The risk to expose the wound and open ourselves to healing. The risk of moving towards the younger brother who hurt us in the possibility of a new beginning.

We don't know what the older brother does. Jesus is inviting us to answer the question for ourselves. But there is one final thing we do know. The father is there, with the older brother. He hasn't left him in the field to decide alone or waste away. The father is there, he always is.

QUESTIONS

1. Which son in the story do you resonate with the most at this moment?

2. Can you think of times you've been the older brother, using control to hide fear?

3. How does your image of God compare to the image of the father? Does God look and act like the father, or does God look and act like you, your traditions, your family of origins, or some other influence?

4. What feels most risky about revealing your wound to the father? Is there a small risk you could try today?

Prayer

God of older siblings, would you confront lies, unravel fear and anger, and tend to wounds? I confess that I can be an older brother. I may not act like the Pharisees, drawing hard lines with religion, but I've excluded, hoarded, and hidden from you, my siblings, and even myself. Would you give me the courage to receive love and pull up a chair next to my siblings, not in contempt or pretense, but in equity and humility. Would you help me risk in receiving what, in you, was always, already mine.

Amen.

FOUR

Prodigal Father

WHEN I WAS a kid, my dad died of cancer. I was too young to really know my dad, so I don't have my own memories as much as I have stories, told enough that they've become a kind of borrowed memory.

I also grew up in Christian spaces where we talked about God as a father a lot. That's a normal and fine thing to do, and we're going to do it in this chapter, but if you've lost a father, then you know how it can get complicated. Sometimes I found the idea of God as a father comforting. It was nice to believe that God stepped into the grief of my story to become what I had lost. I still find that beautiful, though at the same time, fatherhood language in relation to God can feel a bit like Father's Day—a painful reminder of absence. Sure, God is like a father, but God is not *my* dad.

I think many of us reading this chapter have had a similar experience with the use of fatherhood language in the Bible. I bring this up for three reasons: Firstly because, throughout this chapter, we're going to talk about God as a father and

I'm going to tell stories about both my biological dad and my stepdad. Before I do, I wanted to prepare you and acknowledge that fatherhood language can be complicated, painful, and laden.

Secondly, *father* is a metaphor for God intended to help us understand what God is like. It's a beautiful metaphor, but it's also one metaphor among many that the biblical writers employ. God can be like a father, or a mother (Isaiah 49, 66), and God can also be like a lion (Hosea 11:10), a lamb (Revelation 5), a rock (2 Samuel 23:3), an artist (Jeremiah 18:6), a shepherd (Psalm 23), a fortress (Psalm 18:2), a shield (Psalm 3:3), a slice of bread (John 6:51), or a glass of water (Jeremiah 2:13). Metaphors can help us connect with God, but when we overly commit to one metaphor at the expense of the others, we risk displacing God with an idol.

Finally, metaphors borrow from culture but don't necessarily endorse it. To say God is like a father does not mean, for example, that God endorsed the Roman law of *patria potestas* (translated to "power of a father") that gave fathers virtual ownership over their wives and children. I believe God used the metaphor of father in the world of *patria potestas* to present a profoundly alternative picture of God's relationship with humanity.

Whenever we're engaging a biblical metaphor, we should ask both-and questions. How is God both like and unlike a father? What does fatherhood reveal about God and what does it conceal? Believing God is like a father does not mean we have to believe God is like the patriarchal, exclusionary, or coercive visions many of us have received or experienced. God as father enables us to interrogate our own understandings, challenge projections, and even call out manifestations of fatherhood that run contrary to the one revealed in God.

A RENEWED CONVERSATION

With that said, what does the image of the father show us about God? What do we learn about God from the way God is like and unlike fathers? I think this is the most important question we can ask about this parable because, in my opinion, it gets to the heart of Jesus' intention in telling it. Jesus wants to show his audience, and by extension later readers like us, what God is really like.

Jesus' life and ministry were the initiation of a renewed conversation about what God is like. He often says things like, "You've heard it said. . . , but I tell you," (see Matthew 5) as a way of provoking his listeners to consider their beliefs anew. That's exactly what's happening in the parable of the prodigal son. Jesus uses language and characters his audience were familiar with. Talking about God as a father wasn't new to Israel (Isaiah 63:16). But then Jesus does something interesting—he takes that familiar imagery and both-ands it to show us something new, in effect saying, "You've heard that God is like a father, but I'm here to show you a picture of a father that may not look like your image of God."

Because we've already spent a lot of time seeing the father in the narrative of the two previous chapters, this chapter will focus on what we learn about God from the father in the parable. We will engage theological concepts like Trinity, atonement, judgment, and salvation, I hope in a refreshing way. This sets us up for our next section where we will zoom out to see how our entire faith story is like the prodigal son's parable.

DIVINE DANCE OF THE TRIUNE GOD

When the younger son comes to the father and demands his inheritance, what does the father do? He consents. He gives the son what he asks for. He endures the curse and the condemnation and consents to the son's demands. That's probably not what I would have done. If this was my son, I'd say no and send him to his room. The father could have done that, and worse. He could have locked him up and thrown away the key. The father could have dragged his impudent son before the elders of the town, tried him, and then stoned him in a public display with the help of his neighbors. Even though that was the law (Deuteronomy 21:18–21), the father does none of those things. Instead, he consents and allows the son to leave. In the same way, when the older brother refuses to enter the party, what does the father do? He listens and consents. The father invites the son into the party but does not demand, coerce, or make ultimatums.

In the father's consent, we see and learn an *essential, fundamental, foundational* (need I go on) truth: God embodies consent and works consensually. God's being and nature are consensual. It must be so because love is consensual. True love cannot be coerced or forced into existence—it emerges in participation, in the sharing of self and life with the other, in giving and receiving. Love is consensual, and God is love (1 John 4:8). That isn't a fun cliché or a pleasant euphemism. God's very being is love.

Excuse me while I don my professorial cardigan because we're about to get a little nerdy. Christian theology teaches us that God is triune. This is legitimately a confusing and complicated idea that has baffled the minds of our greatest thinkers for two millennia. But simply put, *triune* means God is a community of three: God the Father, God the Son, and God the Spirit.

How can three be one? That is the question. The Greek word used to describe this interrelatedness is *perichoresis,* which theologian Collin Gunton defines as "the mutual indwelling and coinherence of the persons of the Trinity."[1] *Perichoresis* has often been illustrated as a dance in which one partner steps and the other follows. Together, two dancers create one motion by mutually working together. In the same way, God is one through the mutuality of each member. The Father steps, the Son responds, and the Spirit alights in the middle. Each member consents to the other, creating space within themselves to receive, and give, and reciprocate in kind. The German theologian Jürgen Moltmann describes this relationship by saying that each member of the Trinity "comes to [themselves] by expressing and expending [themselves] in the others [through]. . . self-surrendering love."[2]

All of this means, essentially, that God is a community of consensual and mutual love. God's nature is consensual, and God's work is consensual. God works in the world *with* human partners, not in spite of them. God is moved and responds to the free choices we make, which may feel shocking or surprising to you. It might even upset or worry you. Many of us were raised with images of God as totally transcendent ("other") and unaffected by the world. We use words like *sovereign* to describe the way God sits outside of and above human affairs, and words like *immutable* (which means "cannot change") to describe God's nature.

These words are good in theory, but in our need for certainty and control, we can inadvertently limit God. I believe God is impacted by the decisions and actions we make. When we look at the Bible, we see that God accommodates and consents to us all the time. For example, in 1 Samuel 8:5–7, Israel demands a king so that they can look like all the other nations. This is a direct rejection of God's plan and stated intent that God alone would be Israel's king. What does God do? God consents and accommodates. God gives Israel a king and even incorporates monarchy into the divine plan to rescue the world and reveal God's identity. Jesus, in response to us, takes up the mantle of kingship while at the same time radically redefining it in the consensual mutuality of God's being.

God works with us in participatory and consensual ways because God is most interested in us—in reunion and relationship. The father wants all the kids at the table. Consent is essential because it's the only way true love can occur. If the father gives ultimatums to the older son, like "Come inside or you'll never get a penny of my inheritance," the older son might come in, but not freely. His response would not be in love. If he were to respond to an ultimatum like that, it's because he had been coerced, and there's no joy or reunion in coercion.

We've all probably experienced this dynamic for ourselves. We've been to dinner parties that are free and celebratory, and we've been to parties that are manipulative and tense. There's a difference, isn't there? The kind of invitation we receive determines the kind of party we're going to. Or to say it differently, the means are the ends in God. God wants to form a community of love, so God loves. You can't have one without the other.

A FESTIVAL OF DEATH

The ultimate act of consent comes in the father's endurance. The father surrenders himself to the sons and endures their curses, their demands, and their judgment. Episcopal priest and author Robert Farrar Capon describes the parable of the prodigal sons as "an absolute festival of death, and the first death occurs right at the beginning of the story: the father, in effect, commits suicide."[3] In the story it's not a literal death but an arguably even more painful experience. The younger son curses his father and demands his inheritance, implying, "I wish you were dead," and the father consents. The language in Luke 15:12 is literally that the father "divided the life" between them, giving his son the very thing he needed to survive—dying to his own needs, future, and desires, and allowing the son to take it all and leave. In a similar way, when the father endures the rage and fear of the older brother, absorbing the violence of his boy, he metaphorically dies again. The father consents and surrenders to the wrath, pain, and judgment of his sons.

The death of the father is a metaphor that points us toward the real death of Jesus on the cross. In the world of theological and biblical studies, we call the work of Christ on the cross *atonement.*

Biblical scholarship has a lot of atonement theories, because the Bible never explicitly commits to one theory. Instead the writers of the Bible use many different atonement metaphors to describe God's death. Bible scholar Scot McKnight compares atonement metaphors to a set of golf clubs in your bag: you choose the right one for the right moment, but don't overly commit to one at the exclusion of all the others—that's bad for your game.[4]

Here, I want to look at the atonement image presented in the death of the father. When pressed by the Pharisees to explain his own work, Jesus told a story about a father who died for and by his sons. So it's worth pausing to see the atonement as narrated by Jesus. I will break down Jesus' story into three acts, subtitled *absorbs*, *disarms*, and *reveals*.

Absorbs

The father absorbs the curse, the hate, the wrath, the wasted inheritance, and the exclusion of his sons. He doesn't respond in violence or condemnation, and he doesn't lash out or attack them or meet their wrath with his own. Instead, he endures it—he takes all of it into himself, and then he offers them more. He offers more of himself, more of his love, and more of his grace. Atonement means "at one-ment," and in the suffering of the father, we see him making space in himself for oneness with the sons. The image that comes to mind is that of a parent holding their child as they scream and thrash, enduring their reckless blows, taking it into their own body so that the child and others are protected from harm.

The father absorbs the fear and scarcity of his boys, and he also absorbs the loss of wasted inheritance. The younger brother took his father's wealth and spent it on wild and lavish living. When the younger returns, the father doesn't demand it back. He doesn't ask for repayment or restitution; he absorbs it and pays the cost himself. Sometimes, in our atonement theories, like the older brother, we can become so obsessed with that ledger that we turn God into an angry tax collector. "God *must* be paid back," we think. In that theory, Jesus pays God with his own life. But that's not true. Jesus' death isn't paying God back; Jesus is God absorbing *debt*. God doesn't have to pay God back, that doesn't make any sense! The whole point of the story is that God doesn't care about the *debt*, God cares about *us*.

God does not demand repayment. God doesn't need to satisfy wrath. God isn't some archaic deity on the hunt for blood sacrifices to satiate their appetite, even though that's how some atonement theories present God. God does not pour out wrath on God's Son, in the same way the father does not meet the wrath of his boys with his own. No, all the wrath, judgment, and retribution in the story comes from the sons! They impose it on themselves, each other, and the father. They, not him, demand blood and he, not them, provides it.

Disarms

The father consents and absorbs because he loves, that much we get. But does absorbing pain *do* anything? That's a tricky question because love does not control. We don't love because we know everything will work out in our favor. That's not love, that's manipulation. Yet at the same time, love is the only power in the universe capable of producing more love. Consent and absorption create room for our own hearts and lives to be lighted by the love of another.

Nine years after my father died, my mom remarried a truly wonderful man by the name of Mark. I call him Dad. My dad didn't have any children of his own and always told me he was marrying my mom *and* me. He took his role seriously and, to be honest, I made it hell. To be fair to me, eleven has got to be one of the weirdest possible ages to come into a young boy's life. My body and brain were coursing with pre-pubescent hormonal energy (TMI?) and looking for a fight. Just imagine it: I was in middle school, buying T-shirts from Hot Topic because I wasn't sure I could get away with plaid pants and a studded belt yet, and I was listening to Hybrid Theory by Linkin Park on repeat. I was a pop-punk eleven-year-old who hated math and wasn't afraid to say, "You're not my real dad."

At the same time, I was an eleven-year-old who lost his father. I was a bundle of hormones and suffering through legitimate loss. I remember feeling so alien in middle school—which, I know, who doesn't. But it was an alienation compounded by loss. None of my friends at the time had lost a parent. And I didn't have the language yet to name my own grief and dislocation. Pain, confusion, and fear would bubble up, but I didn't understand why, or what to do with it.

My dad stepped into the middle of *that*. I would yell and scream, tell him I didn't want him, tell him he wasn't my real dad. I would storm off in the middle of conversations and slam the door in his face. I would leave, too. I did that a lot. When I was eleven, I ran away, and when I got older and learned how to drive, I would steal the keys and disappear for hours. What's funny, though, is that if you ask my dad what the hardest part of it all was, he'd tell you, "math homework." He'd sit with me for hours most nights, doing math homework and trying to help me understand. Most nights ended the same way: I'd throw a fit and storm off, and then slowly come back to the table to try again. I graduated high school with a 2.1 GPA, which in case you don't know, is very bad, and I only just made it over the line because my dad worked his butt off for me.

My dad absorbed the worst of me. He sat for hours and did math homework. He listened to me scream and shout. He rushed to me when I totaled the car and held me as I shook in fear. My father gave, and gave, and gave of himself until I had exhausted my fear and rage, and then he gave some more. He called me his son and held me in his arms, somehow still delighted to love this boy of his.

Love like that disarms us. Theologian and pastor Greg Boyd compares this kind of love to the martial art of aikido. The word *aikido* is hard to translate into English but it means something like "the way of unifying force." What makes aikido different from other martial arts is that it focuses on using the force and momentum of an opponent against them. In other martial arts, a person uses their own force against an opponent, but in aikido, you *consent* to the force of the other and let it disarm them. They go for a punch, and instead of blocking it with an opposing force, you consent by moving into it and to the side. The force of their punch carries them forward, catching them off guard and disarming them.

In the parable, the father consents to the rage and anger of his sons. He absorbs their force into himself. They throw a punch, expecting it to be met with equal force, but instead the father steps into the punch and absorbs the motion into himself like an aikido master. That's not what they expected, but it's too late—their momentum is too great, so they stumble forward off-balance and off guard, and they fall. It's so disorienting. It's the same thing that happens when someone genuinely says "I'm sorry" in the middle of an intensifying fight. You don't expect that, so your jab doesn't land and the momentum is off. The steam and anger start to dissipate.

Anger intensifies anger. Force intensifies force. On the cross, Jesus absorbed our violence, fear, and anger into himself because he wanted it to stop, and he wanted us to be free. He sees the wounds and fear and creates the space, in himself, for us to calm down, set aside our weapons, and feel safe.

Reveals

Finally, the third act in the death of the father, of the Son, reveals truth. There are three truths I want to focus on here. The first truth is a hard one: the suffering comes from the sons. That does not mean all suffering is simply the product of "bad apples." Nor does it mean the sons are wholly and totally depraved. The sons in the parable represent us—you and me as individuals, and also the collective "us" of humanity.

When we see the younger son curse his father and the older exclude his younger brother, we are seeing a kind of collective story writ small. God gave us, humanity, the world as our inheritance and we—collectively, socially, historically—spent it on wild living. We look around and wonder why the world is hot, blaming God, but never minding the torch in our hand. The younger son left, the older stayed, but both built a life in scarcity and fear.

The sons have caused suffering, their own and the father's. The father endured *their* wrath, *their* fear, *their* pain in the same way God endures *our* wrath, *our* fear, *our* pain. God suffers at our hands and was even murdered by our fear and systems of violence. That is the second reveal.

Brian Zahnd, in his book *Farewell to Mars*, describes the cross as "shock therapy for a world addicted to solving its problems through violence. The cross shocks us into the devastating realization that our system of violence murdered God!"[5] On the cross and in the father, we see the emptiness and devastation of our greatest weapons. God's consent to our control reveals how painful our attempts at control are. Jesus becomes our scapegoat, enduring our self-protection to unmask our lies. As the father endures the anger of the older brother, the lies are revealed. The older brother isn't trying to protect the interest of his father; he's trying to protect himself.

This leads to the final truth revealed, which is that the sons didn't need to protect themselves. The French philosopher and Christian mystic Simone Weil compared grace to gravity because both are experienced in the fall. When the force of our attack is absorbed in love, we become disoriented and disarmed—stumbling over our own momentum—into the beautiful truth that we never had to fight at all. The war was over before it ever began. God chose to lose it so that you and me, and every sibling in between, could be free of it. The younger brother demanded his inheritance, afraid it would run out. The older worked the field, afraid of losing what was his. Both sons are met by the love of the father who gives them more of what they fought so hard to preserve, proving they never had to fight at all.

Beautiful reveals

Before my mom remarried my dad, I'd often imagine what a dad was like. Stories of my real dad would sort of mix with images of men in TV, movies, or books, forming a fantasy father figure that looked like Dr. Seaver from *Growing Pains* and Sirius Black from *Harry Potter*. Pretty cool, huh? In my mind, he was gregarious, yet kind. He was strong, yet tender. He could take anyone in a fight, but never needed to. He was roguishly independent, yet always present to the emotional needs of his family. He was everything a young boy could imagine a father to be, but I think more revealingly, he was everything I wanted to be. My imagined version of my dad was a projection of my desire for self-sufficiency. If I could just be like that, I thought, I wouldn't need a dad.

I curated my image for a long time, taking bits and pieces from whatever I was watching at the time. Sometimes my fantasy father looked a bit like John Wayne, and other times more like Carl Winslow from *Family Matters*. What always stayed the same were the dynamics of independent presence, a kind of controllable connection. That's what TV dads offered kids like me—a form of on-demand relationship that could be turned on and off at our own discretion.

However, that all changed when my mom remarried. Suddenly there was a real person, literally standing between me and the TV, between me and my projections of independent connection. He couldn't be controlled, turned off, or pushed away because he was real, an actual father inviting me into real relationship.

When my dad entered my life, my images of self-sufficiency were disrupted by the presence of a real person. Here in this actual man I was being forced to ask a new question: What do I really want? Do I want the story I've told myself about independence and autonomy, or do I want a dad? Do I want the fantasy or the father?

The revelation of God forces us to ask a similar question. Here is God in the real, disrupting our projections of self-sufficiency with love and welcome. It's a beautiful revelation, but one that can challenge our carefully constructed fantasies. The question to us, as it was for me and the brothers, is *what do we want?*

THE FATHER REDEEMS

The story of the prodigal sons' father does not end in death, but in new life and resurrection. The father rushes to his sons, absorbing their pain, so that he can offer them restoration. Like the parable, the gospel is about more than death—more than forgiveness, even. The good news is life, restoration, and reconnection.

When we talk about the good news of the gospel, words like *saved* or *salvation* can come to mind. What these words mean is complicated because, like *atonement*, they are loaded with significance and often accompanied by a diverse array of metaphors. It's helpful to look at the image of the father one last time to see the good news he offers each son. In the father's restoration of his lost sons, in the healing of broken relationships, and in the celebration, we see vital components of Jesus' work.

Restoration

When the father met the younger son on the road, he clothed him and placed a ring on his finger. Both are signs that the younger sibling is once again a son, fully vested with all the authority and privileges of his sonship. The son had forfeited all his rights to the father's estate when he cursed him and left. It was as though the son had been emancipated from his father; there's no longer a legal connection between the two of them. The father had no obligation to the son—in fact, he's not really his son at all after he left his family. In restoring his son, the father is choosing to take this prodigal back as a son once again.

The apostle Paul loves to describe God's activity with the language of adoption, writing in Galatians 4:4–5, "God sent his Son, born through a woman, and born under the Law. This was so he could redeem those under the Law so that we could be adopted." The son had forfeited his right to sonship, so "under the law" he's not a son, but the father chose to restore him, adopting him back into the family and giving to him the full legal ("under the law") provisions of sonship. The son is fully restored, which is why Paul goes on to exclaim, "Therefore, you are. . . a son or daughter, and if you are his child, then you are also an heir through God" (Galatians 4:7). The younger son is once again an heir, entitled by grace to a share of the inheritance. I think this is one of the reasons the older brother got so angry when the younger returned—he knew what it meant. He knew the younger brother, who "gobbled up the inheritance" was once again an heir with all the rights, privileges, and authority of a son.

Reconciliation

When the father runs to meet his son on the road, the most lavish gesture of grace is not the robe or the ring he gives him, it's the embrace. The son had left with a curse, but the father meets him in a blessing. He hugs and kisses him before he's even had a chance to bathe or clean up. The father is singularly concerned with his son because he wants reunion and relationship; everything else is everything else. *We can figure out the inheritance later. We can pay your debts and talk to the neighbors, but right now I just want to hold you.* "This son of mine was dead and has come back to life!" the father said, "He was lost and is found!" (Luke 15:24).

In the same way, when the father realizes his eldest son is missing from the party, he rushes out to the fields to find him, to invite him back into relationship with himself and with his younger brother. In the very last verse of the parable, the father looks at his eldest son and tells him, "But we had to celebrate and be glad because this brother of yours was dead and is alive. He was lost and is found" (Luke 15:32). Did you notice the change of language from previous verses? Earlier in the parable, the father had declared "this son of mine," but now, he's telling the older brother "this brother of yours" has been found. Reconciliation moves in all directions, restoring our relationship with God and with one another. The father is making his family whole, and that includes both brothers, who are representative figures for Pharisees and "sinners," for Israel and the world, for us and everyone in between.

Reconciliation is at the very heart of the gospel. God wants to restore our relationships to one another. As Paul wrote, "Christ is our peace. He made both Jews and Gentiles into one group. With his body, he broke down the barrier of hatred that divided us" (Ephesians 2:14). Reconciliation does not ignore the divisions or systems of exclusion and oppression that keep people divided. Instead, true reconciliation tears down the barriers of hatred, including the systemic and intuitional expressions of injustice. If these barriers are not removed fully, reconciliation isn't good news—it's just the perpetuation of existing coercive power structures which maintain the "barrier of hatred." True reconciliation is about justice and the healing and wholeness that comes, for both brothers, when the narratives and systems of exclusion are broken down.

Celebration

Finally, redemption includes a party. Each parable in Luke 15 (lost sheep, lost coin, and lost sons) climaxes in a celebration. It's easy to assume the party is an afterlife affair, as if the message is *Someday we will celebrate, but right now we wait.* But in the parable, the party is happening in real time. The father and the son begin to celebrate even while there's still work to do to restore the older brother. This is important for us to understand—the Christian life isn't about waiting for Jesus' return, it is about enacting the party in the here and now. We have been invited into a way of life constituted by the work of the father, symbolized in the party. In 2 Corinthians 5:18, Paul says we've been reconciled and given the work of reconciliation. Just as we experienced the grace of our father, we are invited to extend his gift to the world around us.

Now to say that we're invited to *live the party* does not mean we're supposed to be toxically optimistic people who ignore the difficulties of our world. The party is a symbol of how we live, meaning that our lives can look like a table where everyone is invited to sit. We can live out the hospitality, adoption, and reconciliation of the father, and participate in tearing down dividing walls of hostility. We can celebrate our brothers and sisters, refute our own shame narratives, and practice our welcome. We can burn the ledger and rush into the fields to find our older brothers. We can forgive and be forgiven. To say it simply, the party is a symbol for following Jesus and living in wholeness with the father now.

REDEMPTION FOR ALL

One metaphor that shows up in the Bible to describe God's saving work is *redemption*. Redemption is the idea of regaining possession of something that was lost or sold. In the Old Testament, there were redemption laws so that lost property or valuables could be regained. Say your grandfather made a bad business decision and lost the family farm. In that situation, a family member could purchase the land back and return it to your family at any time. God takes up this metaphor throughout the Bible to describe the way in which God is freeing us from loss and restoring us to our inheritance.

What's interesting about redemption in the Bible, though, is that it's not a one-way street. It's a reciprocal experience. In our parable, the younger brother is redeemed, freed from his debt, and restored to his inheritance. The father too experiences redemption, because he also receives something valuable back—his beloved son. Theologian Bradly Jersak says the same is true of God, explaining, "God experiences redemption, too. Through Christ, he redeems us back to and for himself. We are his own possession, lost for a time, and he has brought us back: 'the redemption of those who are God's possession'" (Ephesians 1:14 NIV).[6] The father celebrates his son because he is glad to receive him back. The party is as much the father's as it is the son's, because it's his time to celebrate and rejoice over the return of his children. This is his moment to experience the good news of reunion, adoption, and reconciliation.

This is what the father has been waiting for, and now he gets to party.

It is easy to focus on the ways in which the sons have cost the father, but the emphasis of the parable is not on how much they've cost the father, but on how much they are worth to him. The father loves his sons and is willing to pay whatever cost to be with them. He doesn't give a hoot about his wasted inheritance; he simply wants his sons. He wants reunion and reconciliation. He wants the family to be made whole. He wants redemption.

The heart of the father is his sons, and the heart of God is us. As we look at the father, we are seeing Jesus' image of God. *This is what God is like.* You may have heard that God is like a vindictive judge, a grizzled warrior, or an absentee parent, but Jesus is showing us that God is like a father whose chief desire is relationship with his children.

When we look at the father, and more importantly, when we look at Jesus, we are seeing what God is like. We're seeing images of a God who loves, who pursues, and who desires relationship. A God who burns the ledger, chases us into the field, and offers us a seat at the table. This is a God who wants to party, who wants to celebrate our return. A God who is more interested in reunion and homecoming than debts, inheritance, or wasted assets. This is what God is truly like.

Jesus gave us this parable to confront and expand our images of God, to show us what God is really like. Because of that, it is worth pausing here for a few moments to ask ourselves, how do we imagine God? The theologian A.W. Tozer once said, "What comes into our minds when we think about God is the most important thing about us. . . We tend by a secret law of the soul to move toward our mental image of God."[7] How we see God will shape our faith and life. Like the sun at the center of our solar system, our image will draw all of life into its orbit. So, what holds the center?

QUESTIONS

1. How does the image of the father in the parable of the prodigal sons fit with your current images of God?

2. Are there features or aspects of your image of God that sit uncomfortably within you? Take a moment to write them out and name them.

3. Where do you believe those images come from?

4. Did you find anything challenging in this chapter? Can you name why?

5. Has your image of God changed or expanded at all from this chapter? If it has, in what ways?

Prayer

God, we have seen that you are like a good father who longs for our return, but if we're honest, it can be hard to believe. Help us today, through your Spirit, experience your welcome. Help us see you so that with the renewed eyes of love, we can critically evaluate all our images of you. And make your love real so that we can know, deep in our bones, that nothing in all the universe could ever separate us from your love.

Amen.

FIVE

Prodigal Story

FOR THE LAST three chapters we have focused on the parable of the prodigal son. We've been meeting the characters, exploring the world, and trying to show how this parable is the gospel in a nutshell. It's not the whole story or the only story, but it is a snapshot of the gospel according to Jesus. In this chapter, we're going to zoom out a bit to look at the broader story of God to see how it is like the parable of the prodigal son.

If the parable of the prodigal son is the gospel in a nutshell, then it should look like the gospel in large. As we zoom out to look at the broader story, we should see similar plot, themes, and most importantly character. If the father represents God, then God should act like the father throughout time and history, right? If the father chases estranged sons into the field and greets long-lost kids on the road, then God too should be on the hunt for us, right? And if the father throws elaborate parties to create environments of celebration and belonging, then God too should celebrate our arrival with an abundant table, right? Right. Right?

Here's the problem. The stories of God we've inherited don't always sound like the stories Jesus told. In Jesus' story, God is a father who loves recklessly, restores lost sons, and throws elaborate parties. But you've probably heard other stories about God that seem to contradict Jesus' story, or at least are hard to square with it. While I was writing this book, I started asking my friends what version of the gospel they had heard growing up. I wanted to know what "good news stories" they'd inherited and how those stories compared to the story Jesus tells. The most consistent answer I heard was "courtroom." The story goes something like this. . . tell me if you've heard it before.

THE JUDGE

You're dead, that much seems clear, but everything else is a bit fuzzy. Before you can get your bearings, you hear a *thud* coming from high above. You look up and see a terrifying and awesome sight. A judge, massive and beyond comprehension, presides. He slams his gavel and says, "We are here to decide your fate. To assess the actions, inactions, and even thoughts of your life to determine your eternity." The judge pulls out a massive file and begins to read aloud. It takes a moment, but you realize he's reading the mistakes of your life, every lie, every shortfall, every iota of imperfection. It lasts for hours, until the judge reaches the final moments of your life, then he shuts the file looks down and asks, "How do you plead?"

What do you say? How do you defend yourself against such a list of abstracted wrongs? Maybe you try to add context to the accusations. But the judge responds, "A sin is a sin is a sin. No matter the reason, it's still a violation of my law." Maybe you try to plead ignorance: "I didn't know, your honor, I tried my best but didn't know the law," to which the judge responds,

"Ignorance is no defense, these laws are absolute." In a final protest you shout out, "This is unfair, unjust! How could I have kept a law I didn't know; how could I have done enough good when you won't even listen to my story?" To which the judge responds, "You couldn't have. All fall short. No amount of good could cover the bad, because you didn't just do bad things, you *are* bad. I have therefore found you guilty! Your life of sin and disobedience has incurred an impossible debt, therefore I sentence you to an eternity in hell."

As the verdict rings in the air, you hear a commotion coming from the back of the court. You turn to see a man rushing to your side like Atticus Finch; he looks at you and nods knowingly, then he approaches the bench. "Your honor" he says, "You have found the defendant guilty, for they are. They have sinned against you and are therefore justly condemned to an eternity in hell. But I have an idea. What if I took their place and paid their debt for them? Would you then relent and allow them into heaven?" The judge considers the proposal and says, "Cool. The debt will be paid, and my wrath appeased." At that, the bailiff comes to remove the man, and, in the rush, you turn and ask him who he is. He looks at you and says, "I am the son of the judge, and now because we have swapped places, you are too." And at that strange, unnerving word, the bailiff leads the son away to suffer on your behalf.

TWO VERSIONS OF ONE STORY

The courtroom imagery stems from a theory of atonement referred to as the penal or legal theory of atonement. The legal theory of atonement developed around the 1500s and gained widespread popularity in the work of theologians like John Calvin and Martin Luther. For Luther, the image of God as judge came as a relief. In his day, the Catholic church was charging money for the forgiveness of sins in a practice called indulgences. As he was reading the Bible, Luther discovered the idea that "Jesus paid our debts" and as a trained lawyer began to apply it, in protest, to the practice of indulgences. It was revolutionary and freeing. We don't have to carry the spiritual or fiduciary debt of sin; Jesus paid it all, God the judge has declared us not guilty!

Most images of the gospel have a context and within their place and time offered good news. Today, however, the legal theory of atonement has come to dominate Western understandings of the gospel—so much so that my friends would name the courtroom as their primary inherited gospel story. And though it was once a liberating image it has, for many, become a terrifying symbol of judgment devoid of grace or relationality. But it's helpful to remember that the legal theory is only five hundred years old, which is relatively young in church history perspective, and is not shared by many Christians today, including within Orthodox and Anabaptist traditions. There is an older and, I believe, more Jesus-centered, apostolic tradition of the gospel we will call the *restorative gospel,* in contrast to the *legal gospel.*

Where the *legal gospel* envisions God as a judge, the *restorative gospel* sees God as a father or physician. Where the *legal gospel* is like a courtroom, the *restorative gospel* is like a hospital or a welcome home party. Where the *legal gospel* understands sin as misdeeds and violations of the law, the *restorative gospel* goes deeper and explains that sin is like a disease or a wound that harms us and others. The *legal gospel* sees Jesus arguing our case before his father the judge, but the *restorative gospel* says God is just like Jesus and together with the Spirit they are working to make a home for you and me.

Here we have two versions of the gospel. Two different ways of articulating the good news story of Jesus. What are we to do with these two stories? I've already played my cards; you know which story I believe is the one closest to Jesus' own. But because the *legal gospel* is such a dominant story, I think it's worth exploring in a bit more depth.

In the following section we will look at the *legal gospel* and identify key features that you're probably familiar with. Then I'm going to ask a few questions. Questions that, I believe, reveal certain problems with the *legal gospel*. These are questions that began to gnaw at me and that led me on a search for a more Jesus-like, biblical articulation of the gospel. I want to be clear here—my goal is not to criticize or shame you or the tradition you come from. The *legal gospel* has sparked faith in millions, and it revolutionized the world in the sixteenth century. I want to honor that while also pressing us towards what I believe is a more Jesus-like gospel.

Once we've explored the *legal gospel,* we will look at the features of the *restorative gospel* to see how it fits within the broader story of God as told throughout the Bible.

LEGAL GOSPEL

What is the broad story of the *legal gospel?* How do we tell it?

- In the beginning, God created humans to glorify God and live in fellowship with God and one another.

- God placed humans in the garden to care for the animals, steward creation, and act as his representatives to the world.

- Something terrible happened. Humans rejected God, and in turning away from God they sinned and became sinners.

- Because God is perfectly holy, just, and righteous, God cannot be in the presence of sin or even look upon it. So God turned away from Adam and Eve and banished them from the garden to bear the curse of sin and death.

- Humans are fundamentally separated from God, and even if we try to please God or justify ourselves before God, our efforts fail miserably. God's disposition towards us is one of enmity. We are enemies of God who must be punished for God to be holy, just, and righteous.

- But thanks be to God! In God's love for us, God sent his son Jesus to stand in our place, live the life we could not live, and suffer the penalty of sin we could not bear.

- God put all our sin onto Jesus and then poured out all wrath and judgment onto Jesus, who appeases God's wrath, satisfies his anger, and satiates divine judgment.

- Because Jesus endured punishment faithfully and without sin, God raised him from the dead.

- Now, if we turn towards God, if we believe Jesus died for our sins, we receive Jesus' righteousness as though it were our own. God can now turn towards us in love, not wrath, because we have received Jesus' righteousness.

- If we do not believe in Jesus, we remain in sin separated from God. God's wrath continues to be aimed at us. If we die unrepentant, God will condemn us to hell to bear the full weight of his wrath for all eternity. God will be forever turned away from us.

- Therefore repent! We must turn towards God to be released of guilt and to experience eternal life.

Theologian Bradley Jersak says the legal version of the gospel can be summarized as, "When you turn from God, God turns from you. If you turn back to God, God will turn back to you."[1] Does this version of the gospel sound familiar? I've heard it a lot, and it was the one I learned to preach and teach. In a way, it's a story I am thankful for, because it had a hand in revealing to me the love of Jesus. But there are some problems I'd like to address.

PROBLEM 1: FLAWS IN THE DEFENSE

The first problem I want to address in the legal story of the gospel has to do with the law and God's nature. According to the *legal gospel* we have failed God's perfect and holy law and are therefore justly condemned to death. But that leads to two questions. First, why did God give humanity a law we were doomed to fail at? It reminds me of the TV show *The Good Place*, where (spoiler!) the characters realize no one has been able to make it to the Good Place in 521 years. It had become impossible to get in—life became too complex, and every good decision was outweighed by a thousand negative implications. No matter how much people grew or matured they always failed to accrue enough good points to make it to "the good place." The same is true in our *legal gospel* story. The law is impossible to fulfill; it's a system that seems to conspire against us. So why give it? Why give a law we are destined to fail? It seems cruel.

The *legal gospel* says the law reflects God's perfect nature. When we sin, we aren't just breaking a law but acting *against* God, and because God is perfect and holy, the punishment for sin is eternal. In this sense, it's not about a cold system but about God's very nature. God is perfect and just and therefore *must* punish sin. But this raises more questions than it answers.

What kind of God "has to" do anything? Is God a slave to God's own nature? It's in my nature to want a burrito, but I can refuse. Can't God? Or does God *want* to judge us this way? Is God a judge above and beyond anything else? Is God more a judge than a father? A shepherd? A friend? The writer behind the book of 1 John says that God is love, but if this story is to be believed, God is a judge first.

Whenever our theories about God say God "must" or "can't," we have entered dangerous territory. God is God and therefore can do anything. But if God "must" punish us because of holiness, righteousness, or justice, then we have made holiness, righteousness, or justice god. If God is God, then nothing limits God accepts God's own choice. That is my first problem with the *legal gospel*—when interrogated and explored, we find an idol at the center.

PROBLEM 2: GOD AGAINST US

The second problem I see in the *legal gospel* is the way it pits God against us. According to the *legal gospel*, God's primary disposition towards us is enmity. When we sin, God turns away and begins to count our sins so that when we die God can bring a case against us. But how can that possibly square with the most famous passage in the Bible, "For God so loved the world" (John 3:16)? And where did we get the idea that God cannot be in the presence of sin? Again, we've run into the issue of saying God "can't" do something, but furthermore, it doesn't make any sense. God sees all, knows all, and is everywhere. That means, one would assume, that God sees, knows, and is in the presence of sin all the time. And if Jesus is God in the flesh, what do we do with all the stories of Jesus being with sinners? The entire Jesus story is about God moving into the neighborhood to be close to us. To be with us, in the full reality of the human experience. In our joy, our beauty, our sin, our wounds, and our victories. If Jesus is God, then God can be in the presence of sin. In fact, in Jesus we see a God who rushes to be with us in our sin.

PROBLEM 3: GOD AGAINST GOD

My final problem with the *legal gospel* is the way it pits Jesus against God. The *legal gospel* says Jesus takes on the wrath of his father to satisfy God's judgment so that we can be forgiven. But why does Jesus have to give his life to his father to save us from his father? This sounds confusing, but is even more convoluted than that, because in Christian theology we believe Jesus is God, one with his Father. Which means the question is actually, "Why does God give God's own life over to God, in order to save us from God?" Huh? Again, this raises so many additional questions. Does God *have* to sacrifice the one and only son? Or is God divided against Godself? Does the God who is Jesus love us but the God who is judge condemn us? Are we loved by a third of God and hated by a different third? (Speaking of which, where's the Spirit?) Or does the sacrifice of Jesus somehow convert the judge? Is that the good news?

GOD LIKE JESUS

How do we discern between these two different versions of the gospel? How do we know which one is a more accurate reflection of the broader, bigger story of God? Well, we look to Jesus. In chapter 1, I argued that the gospel is good news that God is like Jesus. Jesus entered the world to reveal the truth about God. When we look at Jesus, we see the perfect image of (Colossians 1:15) and ultimate revelation of God (Hebrews 1:3). When Jesus eats with sinners, celebrates with outcasts, and challenges

Pharisees, we're seeing the perfect image of God's nature, action, and orientation. When Jesus heals, forgives, and shows mercy we're seeing God heal, forgive, and show mercy. When Jesus tells stories about God as a loving father who rushes to be with his lost children, we are hearing the words of God describe the person of God. And when Jesus dies, consenting to the violence of humanity in sacrificial love, we are seeing God's very self on display. The good news of the gospel is that God is like Jesus and has always been like Jesus.

If we want to evaluate the authenticity of a gospel story, we look to Jesus. Jesus is the framework we use to interpret and understand the broader story. That doesn't mean we know everything with certainty—we're still talking about God here— but it does mean our understanding is grounded in a person who is knowable. Therefore, if our images of God do not look like Jesus, we have a problem. If Jesus loves to be with sinners, then God does too. If Jesus says he is like a physician who has come to heal, then God is like a physician who has come to heal. The *legal gospel* says God turns away from us when we turn away from God, but that cannot be true if God is like Jesus. At every moment, Jesus is God turning towards us. Like a father waiting and searching for his lost boys, God is always for us and always turned towards us.

THE RESTORATIVE GOSPEL

What then is the broader story of the *restorative gospel*? If Jesus is our framework for reading and understanding the story of God, how does our narrative shift? The *restorative gospel* shares certain features with the *legal gospel*, but as we walk through this story, see if you can spot the distinctions. I don't think it will be that hard.

- **In the beginning**. Like the *legal gospel,* the *restorative gospel* starts in the beginning when God creates a world of beauty, life, and light. It's a place teeming with potential, repeatedly called "good" by the Creator. In the middle of this good world, God places us. Humans who are created in the image and likeness of God to live in fellowship with God, self, others, and the created order. As image bearers, we have both an ability and responsibility to represent God in the world by acting like God, curating, and creating in love and generosity. This is how the story begins. Genesis 1 is a poem laden in the grammar of goodness, love, and abundance that presents a picture of a home in which we dwell in loving fellowship with God, one another, and the world.

- **Inciting incident.** Like the *legal gospel,* the *restorative gospel* names that something terrible happens. In Genesis 3, humans turn away from God. Our poetic ancestors, Adam and Eve, reject God, his world, and his way for their own. Like the prodigal son, Adam and Eve demand their inheritance to spend as they see fit.

- **Sin enters the story.** In the immediate aftermath, Adam and Eve hide away from God because for the first time they experience shame. The text tells us that Adam and Eve know for the first time that they are naked, and sew together leaves to cover themselves. Then, when God finds them hiding, Adam and Eve blame one another, scapegoating each other to hide their shame. This story illustrates an important distinction between the *legal gospel* and the *restorative gospel*'s understanding of sin. Where the *legal gospel* defines sin as misdeeds or violations of the law, the *restorative gospel* understands sin to be that which distorts goodness. Before sin, Adam and Eve were unafraid and unashamed, living in harmony with God and one another. But after sin, human relationships experience the effects of shame, fear, and discord. The biblical word used for sin means to "miss the mark." In the *restorative gospel,* the mark is love. Sin is turning away from or rejecting relationship. As New Testament scholar Scot McKnight says, "Sin is the hyper-relational distortion and corruption of [our] relationship with God and therefore with self, with others, and with the world."[2]

- **God's response.** How does God respond? In the *legal gospel,* God turns away. But in the *restorative gospel,* and in the biblical story, God turns towards Adam and Eve. God rushes after Adam and Eve and finds them hiding (like the older brother). God asks them, "Who told you were naked, that your bodies were something to be ashamed of?" Then God does something marvelous. God accommodates their need and clothes them. God makes a promise to partner with them in their healing. And then, as Adam and Eve leave their home to spend their inheritance, God does the most surprising of things. He goes with them. God does not turn away from Adam and Eve but moves towards them, to be with them.

- **The story unfolds.** The Old Testament scriptures cover a lot of ground that we don't have time here to explore. But the story of God continues to unfold in these pages. When Cain kills his brother Abel, God rushes after Cain and confronts his violence, but then commits to protect him and be with him. We could talk about Sarah, Abraham, Moses, or David and show how, when each rejected God, God turned toward them and promised restoration. Or, when Israel rejected God in favor of false idols, God did not give up on them or turn away from them but instead moved towards them. Again and again, God pursued Israel, chose faithfulness, and committed to partner with them for their healing and rescue.

- **Incarnation.** God, who so loves, entered the world to be with us. In the ultimate gesture of "turning towards," God steps into time, place, and reality to reveal love and restore us as image bearers. Unlike the *legal gospel,* the *restorative gospel* sees the entire life of Jesus as a part of the gospel. When Jesus forgives, heals, parties, confronts, rests, sings, eats, and more, we are seeing the gospel embodied. Jesus is God, turning towards us. The one who always moves to be *with*.

- **The cross.** When church and state conspire against Jesus, condemning him to death, what does Jesus do? He consents. Jesus absorbs the violence, hate, and hostility of our world. He takes it all into himself and then does the most surprising of things. He offers more of himself. The *legal gospel* sees the cross as a kind of divine transaction in which Jesus pays the penalty for our sin on our behalf. But God doesn't have to pay Godself back. The courtroom imagery breaks down here and should be replaced with the biblical imagery of redemption. As in the parable of the prodigal son, the father chooses to absorb a loss and never requires repayment from anyone.

- **Resurrection.** Thanks be to God, the power of sin, death, and fear can never overcome the power of God's love. Jesus absorbs violence into himself until it is exhausted and revealed to be empty. Then, as is his nature, Jesus turns towards us again and offers us himself, his life, and his home. God absorbs the loss and forgives whatever debts we've accrued because God is God and there are no limits to God's wealth, abundance, or creative power. Sin, death, and loss can never overcome God.

- **Ascension.** The *legal gospel* stops at the cross, but Jesus' entire life and continuing work are a part of the good news story. After the resurrection, Jesus ascends. This image of him taking up his heavenly throne points to how Jesus has defeated sin, death, fear, and the powers of evil.

- **Pentecost.** Before Jesus ascends, he tells his disciples that he will never leave them as orphans but will send his Spirit to be with them. On Pentecost, Jesus' friends and disciples receive Jesus' Spirit, his very presence within them. Jesus may not be here with us physically, but as is his nature, God has sent the Spirit to be with us—to turn towards us, and to help us experience the goodness and love of our God.

- **Repent.** The biblical word we translate *repent* means to "turn around." Like the prodigal son, we are invited back home. God continues to move toward us, and repentance is the invitation to turn toward God, to receive our welcome at the prodigal party, and to live in fellowship with God, self, others, and the world.

- **In between.** We live in an in-between. God is at work, but that work is not yet finished. The prodigal party has started but there are still siblings in the field. The world still feels the effects of the sin disease. Humans still buy a lie about our worth. We still form institutions and systems of injustice. God's movement towards us does not deny or invalidate our experience of pain, suffering, or difficulty. We live in between. But, within this in-between, we've been invited to partner and participate with God's healing and restorative work. Which means, here and now, we are invited and called to live out the gospel like Jesus. To know him, be with him, and live like him.

- **The end of the story.** Finally, how does the story end? The *legal gospel* ends with death and heaven. But that's not how the biblical story goes. In the book of Revelation, the last book of the Bible, we see a vision of where the world is headed. It's not fire. It's not judgment. It's not destruction or ruin or everlasting torture. It's an image of restoration. We see a picture of the kingdom of heaven coming down to earth, so that our place and God's place will once again be one place. This is the ultimate homecoming, the party to end all parties. This is where it's all headed. This is the mission of God.

Can you spot the difference between the *legal gospel* and the *restorative gospel*? Between the biblical story of God and the ones we often tell? Here, God is always moving towards us. There is nothing—no barriers we could erect, no fall so great, no wall so high—that God cannot and will not overcome to be near us. And just as this is true of the biblical story, it's true for our lives. There is nothing, in all the universe, that God will not overcome to be with us. No matter how many times I turn away from God, God never turns away from me. No matter how many times I doubt, stumble, or just sit on the road and give up, God does not and will not leave. God walks with us, moving at the pace of love, to be near to us.

The apostle Paul declares that nothing can separate us from the love of God (Rom 8:25), And *nothing* means *nothing*. I can reject God's love, but God does not reject me. I can turn away from God, but God does not turn away me. I can run but God will always run after me. I can leave the house, but God will never lock the door.

AN OLD MAN AT THE FIRE

One summer night in 2023, my wife and I were camping with friends at one of those private campgrounds where all the spaces are located uncomfortably close together. It was a little tight, but we'd chosen this site because of its quick and easy access to a reservoir. We tried our best to pretend like we were alone; set up our tents facing away from the RVs, made dinner, then we settled in around the campfire, soothed by the hum of diesel-powered generators.

While we were sitting at the fire, a figure approached. He stood just outside the light of the fire, obscured in the darkness. I'd barely noticed him in my periphery when he spoke up and said, "Hey, I've got more beer than I can drink by myself. Would you come and sit by the fire with me?" I don't know what came over me, but without hesitation I said yes. Maybe my friends felt the impulse too or maybe they're just good sports, but we all left our campsite and headed to his. That's how we met Roy.

Roy had a wild story. He grew up Mormon, left religion, got into some trouble, went to jail, got married, got divorced, had a long-lost child he'd just connected with, broke his back driving a garbage truck off a cliff, and was recently remarried. I was instantly a fan of Roy. He reminded me of the men my father had hung out with who, after my dad died, became a big part of my life. They were an unkempt, rowdy bunch. They were veterans, bikers, and miners who spent their free time breaking horses, fixing classic cars, and putting up with me. They were tough but, underneath it all, tender men. Roy was like that.

We stayed around Roy's fire for a long time. We shared stories, met Roy's new wife, listened to music, and as often happens when you spend enough time with someone, talked about faith. Roy's experience of faith was complicated. After he left Mormonism, he tried out a few Protestant and Evangelical churches but got tired of all the "bulls—" (his word). The more we talked, the more honest Roy got. He shared his frustration with faith and God. He named his doubts, his hopes, and his struggles. He told us he loved Jesus but didn't understand why there was so much suffering in the world if God was good. To which we said, "Us too." He said he loved stories about Jesus, to which we said, "Us too." And he said he wasn't proud of his life but wanted to believe Jesus would welcome him. To which we said, "He does."

When Roy found out I was a pastor he audibly guffawed, laughed, and then jokingly said, "I knew I felt the Spirit." Then he asked me to tell him a story.

"No bulls—, what would you say if I was sitting at your church? Tell me a story about Jesus."

So I did. I told him a version of the story we just walked through. It wasn't eloquent; Roy had just offered me (rather aggressively) a blackberry hard lemonade, and no one has ever been eloquent while drinking a hard lemonade. When I finished, Roy said something that better captured the story I was trying to tell, in fewer words. Roy said, "I want to believe that when I die, Jesus will be there waiting for me. Like an older brother. Like an older man who looks on a younger and says, 'I'm proud of you.'" Then Roy, looking at me and my best friend, said, "Kind of like I see you two young guys."

All I knew to say in response was, "Roy, I believe he will."

Roy then asked if he could give us hug, to which we said yes. Then he told us he loved us and that we were now family. And honestly, I can't think of anything more gospel than that.

THE GOSPEL ACCORDING TO ROY

The gospel is good news. The kind of good news that shows up in the most surprising of places, like around a campfire at a claustrophobically enclosed camp site. The kind of good news that looks at two random men and says, "I'm proud of you." The kind of news that helps us love more, receive more, give more, and become more fully human.

The gospel is for Roy and for you and for me. It is the good news that God loves us, and that, in the words of Paul, nothing can separate us from that love. If the *legal gospel* can be summarized as, "When we turn away from God, God turns away from us," then the *restorative gospel* of Jesus could be summarized, "God never turns away." God is always moving towards us. Always running to meet us on the road or find us in the field. There is nothing that can separate us from God's love. This is God we're talking about after all.

QUESTIONS

1. In this chapter we explored the *legal gospel* and the story of the courtroom. Was that story familiar? How does it make you feel?

2. How did our reading of the *restorative gospel* compare with Jesus' story? Are there any elements you think were missing? Or any questions that still linger?

3. Was there a feature of the *restorative gospel* that stood out to you, either because it was new, refreshing, surprising, or challenging?

4. If someone asked you to tell them the story of Jesus, what would you say?

Prayer

God of restoration, help us understand that you are for us. We've heard so many other stories. Stories that tell us we're rejected, we don't belong, we aren't wanted. We've heard stories that you turn away, that you condemn us, that you don't want anything to do with us until we get our life together. Spirit, confront our false stories with the truth of your good news story. Remind us that you never turn away. Help us understand the height, depth, and width of your love. And give us the wisdom to evaluate all stories through the prism of your son, Jesus.

Amen.

SIX

Prodigal Party

I DON'T MEAN to brag, but I've been to some good parties. Beautiful dinners in secret places, seafood boil graduation celebrations, and backyard weddings that turned into table-top dance parties. I've sabered champagne with a butterknife, cried tears of joy at long-awaited pregnancy announcements, and cooked one hundred pounds of gumbo in the woods. So yeah, I've been to some good parties. But, for completely objective reasons, the best party I've ever attended was my wedding. After the ceremony we celebrated with friends and family until the venue asked us to leave. We danced until it hurt and at one moment my father-in-law was hefted into the sky by my groomsmen and sent crowd surfing around the dance floor to "Sweet Caroline."

Now, you might be wondering why I'm telling you this. It's not *just* because I want to brag. And it's not *just* so that you'll go throw your own party, though I'm 100 percent in support of that. But it's because parties are central to the work and life of Jesus. This is one of those things we miss because we tend to treat Jesus like a sanctimonious religious weirdo, but Jesus loved a party. His very first miracle was turning water into wine so that a wedding party could keep going. And on his travels, Jesus would party with Pharisees, outcasts, tax collectors, and anyone else who invited him. In fact, Jesus partied so much he was accused of being "a glutton and a drunk" (Luke 7:34).

Parties were also recurring images in Jesus' teachings. Jesus told stories about kingly banquets, wedding feasts, and he even talked about throwing parties for the strangest things, like finding a missing coin or a lost sheep (Luke 15)—two things people don't generally celebrate because it would be like inviting your neighbors over every time you found your missing keys.

Parties show up all throughout Jesus' teaching, including in the parable of the prodigal son:

> The father said to his servants, "Quickly, bring out the best robe and put it on him! Put a ring on his finger and sandals on his feet! Fetch the fattened calf and slaughter it. We must celebrate with feasting because this son of mine was dead and has come back to life! He was lost and is found!" And they began to celebrate. (Luke 15:22–24)

To celebrate his son, the father lights the barbecue, invites the neighbors, and turns the music up so loud the older brother can hear it in the fields.

What's the deal? Why does Jesus like to party so much? Why does he tell party stories? And why does he place this absolute rager of a house party at the center of the parable of the prodigal son? New Testament scholar N. T. Wright says,

In telling this story, he [Jesus] is explaining and vindicating his own practice of eating with sinners: his celebratory meals are the equivalent, in real life, of the homecoming party in the story. . . . What is more, Jesus is claiming that, when he does all this, Israel's god is doing it.[1]

When Jesus partied, he was showing us what God is like. When he ate with religious leaders, sinners, and outcasts, he was demonstrating the inclusive nature of God's table. This is who God is, this is what God is like, and this is what God is doing—throwing elaborate parties for estranged sons, celebrating the smallest of victories, and preparing a table for the least likely of guests. Jesus parties and tells stories about parties because a good party is a picture of the gospel. As Brennan Manning, author of *Ragamuffin Gospel,* one of my favorite books about the gospel, writes,

> Through table fellowship Jesus ritually acted out His insight into Abba's [God's] indiscriminate love. . . . The inclusion of sinners in the community of salvation, symbolized in table fellowship, is the most dramatic expression of the ragamuffin gospel and the merciful love of the redeeming God."[2]

BAD PARTIES

Good parties are pictures of the gospel. But not all parties are good. For every great party I've been to, I've attended just as many awkward get-togethers, stodgy corporate events, or weird musical theater after-parties where everyone ended up around a piano singing show tunes (I know, I know, some of you love this kind of party and I love that, for you). Inviting everyone over and having music or food doesn't guarantee a good party.

You can have great food at a party that basically amounts to a sales pitch. And with enough money you can hire Beyoncé to perform at your party, but that doesn't mean people will leave feeling loved. So, what makes a party good? What distinguishes a good party from a bad one?

This is an important question because if the gospel is like a party, we need to know whether the party we're being invited to is good or not. Sometimes our modern gospel feels a bit like a good invitation to a bad party. We come to the party because of Jesus' welcome, only to find an overbearing father who requires Victorian-era-like table etiquette. This is one of the most common criticisms of Christianity today, especially among folks who have been wounded by the church. Maybe they read on the website that "All are welcome" but upon arrival experienced a deeply inhospitable environment. I was a bit hesitant to use "party" language to describe the gospel for this reason. Party language is beautiful, but it's also been malformed and distorted. With hype and fanfare, we describe our churches as a "party," but when people arrive, they experience exclusion, shame, and judgment—aka a bad party. Yet Jesus used party language to describe his work and he knew the difference between a good party and a bad one. He attended both. So, what makes a party good? What distinguishes Jesus' parties from others? To answer that question, we're going to look at a few additional party stories to see what they teach us about the prodigal party.

EXCLUSIVE INVITE

In Luke 7, Jesus is attending a party at the home of Simon the Pharisee. Given the tension between Jesus and the Pharisees, it's kind of amazing Jesus is at this party. It's early in Jesus' ministry but already the Pharisees are publicly criticizing him. And yet, Jesus is there, partying with his older brothers.

While at the party,

> A woman from the city, a sinner, discovered that Jesus was dining in the Pharisee's house. She brought perfumed oil in a vase made of alabaster. Standing behind him at his feet and crying, she began to wet his feet with her tears. She wiped them with her hair, kissed them, and poured the oil on them. (Luke 7:37–38)

We don't know much about this woman. The text says she's "a sinner," which is a pejorative description used generically to describe people who are outside the religious boundaries of Israel. Readers often assume she was a sex worker. Pope Gregory went so far as to say this woman was both a prostitute and Mary Magdalene, which became the popular perspective but has little historical or biblical evidence to support it. We simply don't know who she was or why she is described as a "sinner." She could have been a sex worker—that would have earned her the label of sinner in the first century, and Jesus did spend time with sex workers—but we don't know. And at the end of the day, it doesn't matter. Being referred to as a sinner typically has very little to do with what you've done or even who you are, and more to do with how you're viewed culturally. This is a woman is viewed by the religious elites as "outside the bounds"—she's been written off, pressed to the side, and excluded from the party.

Despite these massive cultural barriers, this woman chooses to enter Simon's home to honor Jesus. This is such a wild risk for her to take. She is a woman in a patriarchal world, stepping into the home of a powerful man who views her as "less than." Yet she takes that wild risk. She enters Simon's home, finds Jesus, and begins to honor him by anointing him with oil and washing his feet. Both actions are cultural expressions of hospitality and should have happened right when Jesus entered Simon's home. Good hosts would do that kind of thing for their guest; remember when Jesus washed his disciples' feet before the Last Supper? What makes this woman's actions peculiar is that everything she does comes from the deepest part of her. She gives him her expensive oil, her tears, and even her hair. These actions may seem strange to us, but they are meant to stand in contrast to Simon, who didn't offer any of these gestures of hospitality.

When Simon see's what's happening, he says, "If this man were a prophet, he would know what kind of woman is touching him. He would know that she is a sinner" (Luke 7:39). The implication here is that a real prophet wouldn't let a "sinner" touch them. Simon doesn't want this woman at his party, and he thinks it speaks poorly of Jesus that he lets her stay and be with him. Simon's party is too exclusive for her and, based on what he's seeing, too exclusive for Jesus. So what does Jesus do?

> Jesus turned to the woman and said to Simon, "Do you see this woman? When I entered your home, you didn't give me water for my feet, but she wet my feet with tears and wiped them with her hair. You didn't greet me with a kiss, but she hasn't stopped kissing my feet since I came in. You didn't anoint my head with oil, but she has poured perfumed oil on my feet." (verses 44–46)

Jesus contrasts Simon's welcome with the way this woman welcomed him. Simon's party probably had great food, beautiful décor, and all the right guests around the table. But it was missing the most important ingredient—real hospitality.

LOVE OF STRANGERS

When I say *hospitality* I don't mean the curated, Instagram-ready images we often think of today, like trendy throw pillows and a charcuterie board to impress your friends (both of which I love). Instead, I'm referencing the ancient biblical concept of hospitality, which has little to do with entertaining friends and everything to do with welcoming others.

The Greek word for hospitality is *philoxenia,* which means "love of stranger." For Jesus, this kind of hospitality is essential to a good party, and it's the very thing Simon's party was lacking. Simon's party was a carefully curated experience. The guest list was deliberate and the seating assignments clear. Everything was crafted for Simon's comfort and reputation, which is why he's so upset at the presence of this "sinner." She doesn't belong.

Real hospitality is about creating spaces where all people belong. You can be invited to a party and yet never feel like you belong there. Real belonging requires adjusting the seating assignments, adding an extension to the table, and deliberately choosing to welcome a guest.

Real hospitality is also about honoring the gifts of a guest. The woman bears gifts that come from the deepest part of her, but Simon doesn't respect this woman or the way she honors Jesus. Her gifts are rejected and demeaned. We see this same thing happen when the gifts of women, especially, aren't respected in places of leadership. Or when we diminish the voice of a person who doesn't fit our categories or look like the people we respect. But Jesus confronts Simon, honoring the gifts of the woman, and in effect saying, "She's the real host here." She is the one who, out of herself, gave a gift that created welcome.

The gospel is like a party where strangers are welcomed, honored, and loved. Nearly every party story Jesus told included the presence of unexpected guests who both confront and challenge our assumptions, expectations, and sometimes even desires. The younger brother is a challenge to the older. The good Samaritan is a challenge to the technically obedient priest and Levite. This woman is a challenge to Simon. Good parties, at their best, tear down barriers of division by creating environments where all strangers (Simon included) are welcomed, honored, and loved.

I've always found it interesting that we don't use the Greek word *philoxenia* today when we talk about hospitality, because we do use its antithesis, *xenophobia*. Maybe it's because we are more familiar with fear than love. Whatever the reason, the gospel confronts our fear of strangers and all the ways we seek to exclude, hide, or uninvite them from our parties. And not simply because it's wrong to treat people this way, though it is, but also because strangers come laden with gifts. The woman in this story carries gifts: her oil, her tears, her hair, her act of sacrificial love, and at the very center of it all, herself. She is a Christlike figure, who enters an inhospitable place to create a new kind of welcome that could have been extended to all. Simon could have received her, and her gifts, and been the better for it. And likewise, Simon could have extended himself and his gifts to Jesus and to others in the same way. There is a kind of beautiful reciprocity in the giving and receiving of gifts at a table. Like the best potluck, we all bring something to share, something of value that can enrich the meal and all who gather.

JESUS' TABLE

On the night Jesus was betrayed, he shared a meal with his friends. It was Passover, a yearly religious holiday to celebrate Israel's deliverance from Egypt. Jesus began the meal telling his friends, "I have earnestly desired to eat this Passover with you before I suffer" (Luke 22:15). This moment is so human, so real. Jesus knows what is coming and longs for the safety and intimacy a dinner party with friends can bring.

Jesus takes the bread and the cup saying, "'This is my body, which is given for you. Do this in remembrance of me.' In the same way, he took the cup after the meal and said, 'This cup is the new covenant by my blood, which is poured out for you'" (Luke 22:19–20). Jesus takes the elements of the meal and says, "These are expressions of my love. Signs of my work and an invitation to you." He then commands his disciples to continue eating and drinking this meal in remembrance of him.

As a final symbol, expression, and gesture of his work, Jesus gave a meal, a dinner party. This meal became the defining practice of the early Christian church. In the third century, with the legalization of Christianity in Rome, the meal was formalized to efficiently administer the elements to new Christians, becoming what we call, depending on your tradition, communion, eucharist, or sacrament. But in the early days, it was just called Jesus' meal. And as Jesus instructed, whenever the church would gather, their activity would center on a table and a meal. They would sing songs, read letters, discuss the teachings of Jesus, pray, and address needs, all while sharing food and drink.

In giving the church a meal, Jesus was providing us a way to practice the gospel. In our table fellowship we regularly enact the parable of the prodigal son. At the table, divisions are torn down, hierarchies dismantled, and siblings reconciled. We give and receive forgiveness. We honor gifts, rearrange seats, and learn to belong together. It won't be a tidy or orderly affair—there are kids running loose, loud music playing, and too many servings of potato salad. But that's the point. The gospel has never been about good behavior or well-mannered children. It is about practicing and receiving a love that's big enough to hold all the estranged siblings together.

The problem is that our gospel celebration, our table practice, often becomes self-serving. Like Simon, we host exclusive events for a limited few. There's another party story, in 1 Corinthians 11, in which the apostle Paul offers sharp words to a local church that had forgotten the purpose of their party. He says, "When you meet together as a church, I hear that there are divisions among you, and I partly believe it. . . when you get together in one place, it isn't to eat the Lord's meal" (1 Corinthians 11:18–20). The local church was gathering and eating a meal, but Paul says the meal is no longer Jesus' because there are "divisions" among the believers. Paul goes on to express what those divisions were:

> Each of you goes ahead and eats a private meal. One person goes hungry while another is drunk. Don't you have houses to eat and drink in? Or do you look down on God's churches and humiliate those who have nothing? What can I say to you? Will I praise you? No, I don't praise you in this. (verses 21–22)

We need a little context to understand what's happening here. The church in Corinth was an economically diverse group of people. That is the beauty of the gospel: it brings diverse peoples together around one table. But in Corinth the wealthy, who had comfortable lives and controllable schedules, could arrive at the Jesus meal early, while Christians who labored in the fields were unable to arrive until after dark. When the wealthy and the privileged arrived, they would eat the food and drink the wine, leaving little for others. Instead of a meal, the wealthy had made Jesus' table into a private celebration. Sure, the poor could come, but by the time they arrived, the party was over and all that was left were the scraps.

In response, Paul offered a powerful rebuke: "This is why those who eat the bread or drink the cup of the Lord inappropriately will be guilty of the Lord's body and blood" (verse 27). This meal was supposed to be about practicing the "body and blood of Jesus," giving and receiving the other-oriented, sacrificial love of Jesus. But in their wealth and privilege, people had distorted the meal into a self-centered farce. The issue was even more serious in Corinth, because the meal was an important source of provision for poorer members of the community. When the rich would eat all the food, they were condemning poorer members to hunger and even death (verse 30).

YOUR TABLE IS TOO SMALL

Sometimes when we talk about creating spaces of belonging, especially in places of power, we use the phrase "seat at the table." Like, "We want to make sure everyone has a seat at the table," or "Women need to have a seat at the table." It's a good impulse, but it also belies a problematic fact about some of our parties and tables—they were designed with too few seats. Simon's party had too few seats. There is no room for the woman. So Jesus turns away from Simon's party, and towards her. In the same way, the church at Corinth had too few seats around their table. A party that was built for everyone had become a private affair for a few, to which Paul said they were "guilty of the Lord's body and blood." Paul's words are so sharp because the church had re-established the structural inequalities Jesus' meal was teaching them to tear down. Instead of experiencing and practicing the unity of Jesus' love, the church was divided by class, privilege, and status. Their meal looked like every other bad party.

The gospel is a party that confronts our power, privilege, and position. Because Jesus wants to party with all of us, he is unwilling to perpetuate exclusive affairs that seek to privatize his presence or limit access to him. But I believe Jesus is also uninterested in simply adding a few seats to already broken tables. His party is meant to transform older brothers, not force everyone to conform to their demands. Jesus' party, his table, is for unnamed women with beautiful gifts, younger brothers who barely made it home, and laborers who need a meal after a long day's work. It is also for older brothers like me and Simon who have long sat at tables designed for our comfort. But Jesus' party is a challenge for us older brothers, because it confronts our tendency toward exclusion, comfort, and privilege. As Jesus said elsewhere, "Those who are last will be first. And those who are first will be last" (Matthew 20:16). Like the rich younger ruler who came to Jesus asking what he must to do to be saved, many of us older brothers walk away sad, because we have "many possessions" (Matthew 19:22) we are not ready to give up.

Jesus' meal is the practice and expression of a new world, a new home, in which you and me and everyone in between are invited to belong together. The beauty of the gospel is the way it disrupts divisions; as Paul writes, "There is neither Jew nor Greek; there is neither slave nor free; nor is there male and female, for you are all one in Christ Jesus" (Galatians 3:28).

That doesn't mean difference is erased, but it does mean disparities are undone. It won't always be easy. Parties can be risky and messy affairs, but the good news of Jesus' invitation is that we're all invited, and the very thing we need most can be found inside the party.

A SHORT KING IN A TREE

Jesus was invited to a lot of parties, but one of my favorite party stories comes in Luke 19, where Jesus unceremoniously invites himself to a party.

In Luke 19, Jesus has just arrived at the town of Jericho where a man named Zacchaeus lives. Zacchaeus is a tax collector in charge of other tax collectors, which means he is very wealthy. Luke also tells us that Zacchaeus is a bit of a short king and needs to climb a tree to see Jesus on the road. While walking on the road, Jesus sees Zacchaeus and says, "Zacchaeus, come down at once. I must stay in your home today" (verse 5). Zacchaeus is happy to oblige (verse 6) but the crowd, upon witnessing these events, "grumbled, saying, 'He has gone to be the guest of a sinner'" (verse 7).

Tax collectors worked for Rome and oversaw the taxation of occupied peoples. They were considered traitors and conspirators who had turned against their neighbors for profit. It was a rough job, but it had benefits—tax collectors could siphon a percentage of revenue for themselves. This was how tax collectors were paid. It was a little nefarious but technically legal, which is why people hated them. Zacchaeus, however, wasn't an ordinary tax collector; he was over other tax collectors, making him the *little* point of a very profitable pyramid scheme.

Tax collectors were reviled by their Jewish neighbors, but I want to add a little nuance to our understanding of them.

When we talk about tax collectors, we often envision scummy, greasy, underworld characters. But tax collectors operated within the law and were government employees. Their source of income seems strange but isn't much different than being paid on commission or receiving a bonus if you saved the company money. Tax collectors probably believed they were performing an important service. Taxes paid for things like roads and water, and their small percentage enabled them to continue their work of enabling those services. That's why I love tax collectors in the biblical story; they are relatable. Which is also what makes Zacchaeus's transformation so challenging.

Luke doesn't include many details about Zacchaeus's party. It's a hastily thrown-together event in response to Jesus' abrupt self-invite. But something happens around Zacchaeus's table that leads him to stand up and say, "Look, Lord! Here and now, I give half of my possessions to the poor, and if I have cheated anybody out of anything, I will pay back four times the amount" (Luke 19:8 NIV). At this party, Zacchaeus encounters a kind of abundance that challenges his wealth, privilege, and power. At this table with Jesus, Zacchaeus is transformed.

TRANSFORMATIVE PARTIES

The gospel is a party that transforms us. We experience the generosity of Jesus, his gift of himself, and we become generous. We encounter his love and learn to love ourselves and others. Jesus confronts the ways we exclude, hide, and isolate from others. He challenges our privilege, power, and fear of others. But then, and always, he offers us a home. In fact, the challenge and the invitation are one and the same. As Paul once wrote, it is the kindness of God that leads us to repentance (Romans 2:4). Repentance means to "turn," to think differently, to come home. Like the younger brother on the road or the older in the field, it is the father's goodness and abundance that leads to homecomings.

Zacchaeus experiences the goodness of Jesus' table and is transformed by it. He lays down his privilege and wealth, acknowledges unjust business practices, and seeks repair. Zacchaeus chooses to give away half of his possessions and pay back to all he has taken from "four times the amount" he stole. That is no small feat. As the head of tax collectors, Zacchaeus could be talking about thousands of people. He is like a one-man government issuing reparations to the occupied peoples of Jericho. What a transformation. Zacchaeus sees and acknowledges his sin, the ways he's exploited and horded and the ways his wealth and privilege have excluded others from the table, and in response he throws a party of repair and restitution.

The gospel confronts us and transforms us and, as it does Zacchaeus, invites us to participate in the ongoing transformative, healing work of Jesus. Henri Nouwen in his book about the prodigal son writes, "I now see that the hands that forgive, console, heal, and offer a festive meal must become my own."[3] Jesus is inviting each one of us to become like him; party hosts, partygoers, and party crashers who extend his healing, consoling, forgiving meal to others. In our transformation we become participants in his transforming work.

PRODIGAL PARTIES

Throughout the gospel according to Luke, we find ten party stories in which Jesus attends, hosts, or crashes a party. That number doesn't even include Jesus' party parables, like the three found in Luke 15 (lost coin, lost sheep, lost sons). I wish we had time to explore all of them because they each uniquely contribute to our understanding of Jesus. But what we see in the three stories from this chapter is that Jesus loves a good party because a good party is a picture of the gospel. Good parties are places of hospitality where the least likely are welcomed and celebrated. Good parties are places of equity and inclusion, where tables are redesigned so that everyone has a place of their own to belong. And good parties are places of transformation, where in our experience of generosity, we become truly generous.

Jesus' parties help us understand and imagine the party at the center of the parable of the prodigal son. The father's party, like the Jesus parties, is one where children are welcomed, exclusion confronted, and lives transformed by the generosity of love. As we see and experience the Jesus party, we're invited to party with him and like him.

The Jesus party is not just a future event, though there is a future component. It is a here-and-now kind of party. Besides party, Jesus liked to describe his work using "kingdom" language and would often say things like *the kingdom is here*; *the kingdom is in your midst*; *the kingdom is arriving*. Jesus' party, his kingdom, is here now. There's still work to do and guests to invite, some older brothers are still in the field and a few younger still on the road, but the party has begun. The Jesus party is in our midst, and we are invited, right here and now, to participate. That is why Jesus gave us a meal as the chief symbol of his work. Empowered by his example, we can gather at tables, celebrate the stranger, confront sin, learn to love, be transformed by the goodness of God, and extend Jesus' welcome to everyone right now. Jesus' party is good, so let's go throw a few good parties.

QUESTIONS

1. In this chapter we have explored what makes a good party. What do you think are the essential elements of a good party? Did we miss anything that you think is important to include?

2. How do Jesus' parties (the ones he attended and the ones he talked about) shape, challenge, or change your understanding of the gospel?

3. In what ways can you join with Jesus and party like him in your everyday life?

Prayer

God of good parties, help us party like Jesus. We've seen that you are at work, throwing the best party where everyone is welcomed, included, and transformed. But we confess that our parties don't always look like yours. We curate guest lists for our own comfort and reputation. We sit in positions of honor, ignoring the gifts and worth of others. Confront our parties with the wild goodness of your own. Please expand our tables so that everyone has room to belong. Turn our water into wine because our party has gotten a little stale and we need you to turn up.

Amen.

P.S. We ran out of ice.

SEVEN

Prodigal Belonging

I'M THE YOUNGEST of three siblings. My brothers come from my biological father's previous marriage and are nearly fifteen years older than me. Jake is my half-brother. Mike was the son of my father's first wife whom he adopted, making him my adopted stepbrother. After my father died my brothers stayed around for a while, living with us on and off and spending occasional holidays with us, until I was about ten. Then they disappeared. They stopped calling and visiting: no more holidays, no surprise drop-ins, nothing. Without a word of warning, they were gone, and they stayed that way for a long time.

When adults vanish, childish imaginations do wondrous things to fill the hole left behind. Maybe that's why kids love magic; they're already skilled at graciously suspending disbelief for the sake of the performance. And I did just that. My brothers became characters larger than life. Cowboys, bikers, adventurers. The best a ten-year-old raised on westerns and kung fu movies could conjure. When I got older my imagination became less wild, but no less vivid. I hung photos of them on my walls and imagined them aged, with families of their own but more or less unchanged.

As a teenager I hoped they would return. When I entered my twenties, I nursed the fantasy they would show up for a special event like my graduation or wedding. In my late twenties I hoped for a letter, an email, a Facebook message. By the time I entered my thirties, I stopped expecting a reunion. I wasn't bitter or sad, just resigned to the apparent fact that my brothers were gone. That was, until they weren't.

Twenty years after my brothers disappeared, my half-brother Jake reached out to my mom. He called her one morning because he was in town for a wedding and said he'd like to see us. It was a Sunday, around 10:30 a.m. My mother was at church. My church, where I pastor. She stepped out to take the call while I was teaching. When I finished, I walked to the back and my mom approached, visibly flustered, to tell me, "Your brother just called, he's heading here, right now. He wants to see you." Some thirty minutes later, he reappeared. What a magic act.

It feels cliché to call our reunion surreal, but I don't know another word to describe the experience. There he was, at my church, standing with my mom off to the side. I only knew it was him because he was with my mom. On any other day, in any other situation, he could have been anyone else. He didn't look like I imagined. Not unrecognizable, just unexpected. We talked for a few minutes and then decided the best course of action would be to have a meal, so we left the church for a Mexican restaurant down the street. There it was, the reunion I'd never imagined. My mom, my brother, and me eating enchiladas on a Sunday afternoon at a Mexican restaurant named after a colorful lizard. There was no grand explanation, no emotional reconnection, no apology, no heroic stories. It was nothing I could have predicted; it was strangely normal; it was incredibly awkward—my lost older brother had returned, and it was weird.

It's hard for me to imagine what my brother thought as he returned. I don't understand why he called when he did. Why this visit incited our reunion. What he saw when he looked at his younger brother, now twenty years older. How his body experienced our hug. Did he know he was wanted? Did he know that I'd dreamed of this reunion for twenty years? Had he? Did it fit his expectations? Or unravel them in the regularity of it all? Did he feel like he belonged? Like he could belong?

Jesus doesn't tell us how long the prodigal son had been gone. It's a small detail left absent, maybe for the sake of our stories. I always imagined it as a short period of time, but after the return of my brother I began to wonder if Jesus had a longer time frame in mind. It can take a while to liquidate your assets and spend them. A year? Two years? Twenty? Which makes me wonder what the return of the prodigal was like. Was he recognizable? Did he resemble the young man who left? And what did he experience? Did the fields smell the way he remembered? Was everything like it was when he left? Did he recognize the face of the father hurtling towards him? Whatever the time line, I think we can say with some certainty that the experience would be surreal. It would be strange for a family to receive back their lost son, but it might be even stranger for the lost son to receive their welcome.

LEARNING TO BELONG

Coming home can be hard, but staying home can often be just as difficult. The next time I saw my brother Jake was for

Christmas. I, my wife, my stepdad, my mom, and my brother all stayed together at my parents' home on Christmas Eve so that we could spend Christmas Day together. It was wonderful, but can you imagine how weird that must have been for Jake? Not only was he relearning relationship with me and my mom but he was meeting my wife and stepdad for basically the first time. We have rituals, traditions, inside jokes, and unassigned assigned seats at the dinner table. Every Christmas morning, we eat what my wife lovingly calls "egg fart soufflé," in the afternoon we eat chili (really doing a number on our bowels), in the evening I make dinner, and somewhere in between there's a Nerf war punctuated by my mother shouting about the glassware. These are beautiful things, all of which Jake was invited to participate in, but they also require a kind of learning. And the same was true for us. If we really wanted Jake to be a part of our lives, we had to learn his rituals, traditions, and habits. That might mean our meals become less farty, our jokes less exclusive, and maybe even that our unassigned assigned seats get reassigned so that our place can also become his place.

Homecomings are beautiful but they require this kind of learning, unlearning, and relearning. Or maybe it would be better to say, they require practice. That's not because we need to "practice" to be good enough to belong. Nor do we need to learn the right table manners, etiquette, and vocabulary to belong. Homecomings require practice because even when we're wanted and even when we want to be at the table, it can take time and practice to accept the truth that we are wanted. That we belong. That we are loved.

I think this is what growth, maturity, or (to use a very Christian word) discipleship is. It is the process of learning that we belong. Jesus told his followers,

Are you tired? Worn out? Burned out on religion? Come to me. Get away with me and you'll recover your life. I'll show you how to take a real rest. Walk with me and work with me—watch how I do it. Learn the unforced rhythms of grace. I won't lay anything heavy or ill-fitting on you. Keep company with me and you'll learn to live freely and lightly. (Matthew 11:28–30 *The Message*)

To mature in faith is to walk with Jesus into rhythms of rest, health, and love. Faith is learning to feel comfortable enough in your own skin and love that you can put your feet on the table, slouch deep in your seat, joke with your siblings, and even break the crystal and spill wine on the carpet without fear of rejection. The practice of the Christian life is not about becoming good enough to belong but about developing a kind of intuitive understanding that our belonging was never in question. This table is for you and me, and all our rituals, traditions, inside jokes, and farty food are about creating a space of welcome. But if you don't like chili, that's okay. We'll make what you do like and share it together.

FAITH IS RISK

Practicing belonging is a strange idea. How do you practice what is already true? It's a good question and expresses the paradox of Christian life. We are loved—we do belong—and yet we don't always feel loved, nor do we always live like we belong. I wonder if that's why Jesus told his disciples to become like children. Children have and are something that adults must relearn. Where kids run, adults walk. Where kids jump, adults carefully descend. Children will risk body, heart, and mind for what they want until the world, their experiences, or the asphalt turn them into risk-averse adults.

Faith is like that. Homecomings, reunions, and Christmas dinners with estranged families are all risks. Receiving and giving love are risks. Entering a party where you'll come face to face with the younger brother is a risk. Choosing to see your sibling as the Father sees them is a risk. Choosing to see yourself as the Father sees you is a risk.

STEP BY STEP

Through careful practice and slow time, we acquire an imagination for the love of God, self, and others. We take risks like offering prayers, forgiving our siblings, slouching in our chairs, telling our stories, and in the creative and generative power of love, we come to know our belonging.

The desert father Abba Moses once said, "Everything we do, our every object, is undertaken for love. This is why we take on solitude, fasting, vigils, work. . . for this is why we practice the reading of Scripture, together with all the other various activities. . . we do so to rise step by step to the high point of love."[1] The very purpose of Christian practices is to rise, "step by step," into love. Just as the younger brother puts one foot in front of the other on the road to his father's house, we rise towards God, self, and others one step at a time.

Growth happens at the speed of love. Theologian Kosuke Koyama, in his book *Three Mile an Hour God*, writes,

[God] walks "slowly" because he is love. If he is not love, he would have gone much faster. Love has its speed. It is an inner speed. It is a spiritual speed. It is a different kind of speed from the technological speed to which we are accustomed. . . . It is the speed we walk and therefore it is the speed the love of God walks.[2]

Jesus is unhurried. He invites us to walk with him and "learn the unforced rhythms of grace."

I wish belonging was an instantaneous sensation, but I think it takes time because we have learned, habituated, and acquired a way of living that is often in tension with belonging. The author Henri Nouwen in his own book about the prodigal son wrote, "The farther I run away from the place where God dwells, the less I am able to hear the voice that calls me the Beloved, and the less I hear that voice, the more entangled I become in the manipulations and power games of the world."[3] Outside God's presence we develop skills like self-sufficiency and independence that are helpful tools for self-protection but barriers to the kinship of the table. The closer we move to the voice that calls us beloved, the clearer we see and the freer we become. But the power games and manipulations of the world do not immediately lose their hold on our lives.

The biblical word we could use to describe this is *sin*. In previous chapters we defined sin as missing the mark and that's true, sin is missing the mark of love. At the same time, the biblical writers talk about sin as a deeper reality that infects our minds, bodies, and world. The Bible scholar Douglas Campbell describes sin as an addiction, which is a helpful way of reframing our understanding of sin.[4] Throughout the Bible, sin is described less as moral infraction and more like a disease, an addiction, or even a wound. Theologian Brad Jersak powerfully articulates this:

> The New Testament treats sin as a problem profoundly worse than law-breaking misbehavior. It's a malady with much deeper roots than misdeeds (though these are its ugly symptoms). "Sin" is a fatal disease that cannot be healed by

striving to overcome it or attempting to punish it out of our nature. That would be like a parent whose baby is dying of meningitis urging the child to will its fever away or even trying to spank the virus out of her.[5]

This doesn't justify sin, but it does give us a different way of viewing it. This is important to talk about because sin as woundedness can help us understand why belonging can be so hard to experience. But to talk about sin as wound, addiction, or disease, we first need to address a different way of understanding sin that is prominent in many of our evangelical traditions. As we do, we will find that the way Jesus and the writers of the Bible view sin is often very different from the way we do today.

ORIGINAL SIN

Popularized in the fourth and fifth century writings of Augustine of Hippo, *original sin* is the idea that humans are born sinful, having inherited a sinful nature from our spiritual ancestors, Adam and Eve. This means (1) we are born guilty because of the sins of our ancestors, and (2) our nature has been corrupted by sin. Due to Adam's original sin, we are trapped; guilty in our associated genealogy and enslaved by our genetics.

Whether or not Augustine intended this to happen, the idea of original sin has had a profound impact on Christian self-understanding. We are not simply people who do bad things, according to this theology, we *are* bad. This is why the hymn writer Isaac Watt would passionately ask, "Alas and did my Savior bleed? For such a worm as I?"[6] Or why the famous preacher and nineteenth-century revivalist Charles Spurgeon once wrote, "I feel myself to be a lump of unworthiness, a mass of corruption, and a heap of sin," referring to himself as "all rottenness, a dunghill of corruption, nothing better and a great deal worse."[7] If you grew up in evangelical churches, you're probably familiar with this kind of thing. It's almost like, the worse we see ourselves the holier we are. And by "almost like" I mean exactly like. J. D. Greear, the former president of the Southern Baptist Convention, once said, "One of the surest signs that you've never met God is that you feel pretty good about yourself."[8] Greear believes that if we had really met God, we would know the truth about ourselves, and feel bad. We'd see ourselves as God does—as worms. The famous pastor John Piper says God finds the idea of relationship with us "thoroughly unpleasing"[9] and only begins to delight in us when we change through the power of the Spirit.

Krispin Mayfield, in his wonderful book on spiritual attachment, calls this dynamic "shame-filled spirituality," writing,

> Shame-Filled Spirituality puts us in a terrible place where we actually feel better when we're distant from God and feel worse about ourselves when we're close. Yet, we also need closeness, so we're caught in a terrible dilemma. Though we long to draw near to God, as we come closer, we can only see disgust in the eyes of the Divine, a nettling feeling that we need to become a little bit better, a little holier if we're really going to be liked. And if that doesn't work, we can acknowledge outright that we aren't lovable and we don't expect true closeness until we've completely changed.[10]

Closeness is conditioned on change. We believe God may love us, but we're left with a sinking feeling that God doesn't like us very much.

Is that true? Do we have to utterly hate ourselves to approach God? Is God so repulsed that relationship with us is "thoroughly unpleasing?" When a parent treats a child in this way, we call it wrong, or at least we should. It's a breeding ground for shame and anxious attachment. We know that children grow into health when they are consistently met with steadfast love and affection, not disappointed repulsion. Why would that be any different with us?

ORIGINAL SIN VS. GENERATIONAL SIN

Theologically speaking, this understanding of sin brings up two key issues. The first has to do with us and our nature. *Original sin*, or at least this version of it, posits that humans are bad at birth, guilty of Adam's sin and genetically preordained to it. Our nature, our fundamental self, is sinful. But that is not the story of the Bible. The Bible says we are created in the image of God and named good by our creator. Our truest and most fundamental self is one of love, goodness, and capability. Humans can sin, most certainly, but nowhere do the writers of the Bible argue that we are born guilty. In fact, they critique this very kind of thinking. The Old Testament prophet Ezekiel makes this very clear in a profound moment, writing:

> The word of the LORD came to me: What do you mean by repeating this proverb concerning the land of Israel, "The parents have eaten sour grapes, and the children's teeth are set on edge"? As I live, says the Lord GOD, this proverb shall no more be used by you in Israel. Know that all lives are mine; the life of the parent as well as the life of the child is mine: it is only the person who sins who shall die. (Ezekiel 18:1–4 NRSVue)

The proverb references the lie of inherited guilt, original sin, and God says, don't perpetuate this among my people! Then the prophet goes on to say, "The person who sins shall die. A child shall not suffer for the iniquity of a parent nor a parent suffer for the iniquity of a child; the righteousness of the righteous shall be their own, and the wickedness of the wicked shall be their own" (verse 20). God, through Ezekiel, is directly challenging the premise of original sin; we are not guilty nor will we be judged because of the "iniquity of our parents."

The second question the concept of original sin presents has to do with our orientation. Are we *oriented* towards sin because of our relation to Adam? This is a more interesting question, because it begins to scratch the surface of something we experience. Before we look at the issue underneath the surface, it's important to say we are not broken by the sin of our ancestors, nor are we destined to make their mistakes. As the prophet Ezekiel named, each person is responsible and accountable for their own lives. But if we press into this question a little deeper, we can say that we are affected by the sins of our ancestors. Their decisions do not change our being—of love, value, and goodness—but they do shape our world.

Instead of using the language of *original* sin, the biblical writers prefer the more nuanced concept of *generational sin*. The two ideas share some commonalities in that each speaks of a kind of inheritance. Where they diverge is in the specificity of the inheritance. Unlike original sin, generational sin is the idea that we inherit not a nature, but a story. We live in the wake of our forebears, for good and ill, and contend with the consequences of their lives. Generational sin is a historical inheritance in which we, the inheritors, are bequeathed the whole and holes of life. This kind of sin is not about guilt or being, but about the world we find ourselves in.

We're not guilty because of our parents' (or Adam's) sin, but we are impacted by the stories of their lives. We carry in us memories of their decisions or indecisions, actions, or inactions. This is true for all sorts of things—yes, the pain, but also the good, the beautiful, and the weird. I am a carrier of my mother's dreams, values, courage, and whether I like it or not, idiosyncrasies. Sometimes when my mother says something she thinks is funny, she'll lightly drum on a surface. It's this little endearing quality we all poke fun at, but then the other day my wife caught me doing the exact same thing. Along with the silverware comes an inheritance of habits, histories, gifts, and debts that are ours to parse. Our history does not condemn us or destine us, but it does shape us. We are products of place, time, and people—an amalgam of all that has come before us. We are not destined to repeat the sins of our fathers, but we are vulnerable to their legacy. We do not inherit the guilt of ancestors, but we do live in the world they made.

Generational sin is the recognition of a story, ours, and our families. Unlike *original sin*, it offers a compassionate perspective on our lives. Original sin argues that we are the reason we sin—we are bad and therefore do bad—whereas generational sin recognizes that we have experienced sin. Like the older brother, we have suffered a loss and inherited a story.

A modern concept that can help us understand generational sin is the idea of trauma. Trauma scientist Bessel A. van der Kolk, in his book *The Body Keeps the Score*, writes about the way trauma continues to impact our lives, long after the event took place.

We have learned that trauma is not just an event that took place sometime in the past; it is also the imprint left by that experience on mind, brain, and body. This imprint has ongoing consequences for how the human organism manages to survive in the present. Trauma results in a fundamental reorganization of the way mind and brain manage perceptions. It changes not only how we think and what we think about, but also our very capacity to think.[11]

Traumatic events and experiences, the ones we know and the ones we inherit, can leave an impression on our bodies and psyches, shaping how we perceive and think. We learn ways to survive, what we might call coping behaviors, that have helped us navigate our experiences. Those coping behaviors may not serve us well—they may isolate, hurt, or hinder our healing—but they came from a real wound. Like the older brother, we adopt ways to manage loss. We work hard, grasp for control, medicate to ignore, hide away, but the root of it isn't our "badness." It's loss.

WEAK IN THE KNEES

In 2019, during my second run on the first day of the season, I tore my anterior cruciate ligament (ACL) skiing. I can admit I was being a little reckless. As I was racing down the mountain I attempted a hard turn to the right, but physics can be a real jerk, and instead of turning right, the inertia of my body kept to its previous course. I tumbled over my skis and down the mountain for about fifteen feet before I slid to a stop. I knew something was wrong, but I wasn't sure how wrong until I tried to stand up. As soon as I placed weight on my left leg I heard, audibly, a cacophony of popping, like the noise inflatable package bubbles make when you squeeze them. My knee seized in pain, and I fell back down. As the sensible person that I am, I thought maybe I'd try again. So I gathered myself and tried one more time to the same effect: popping, pain, fall.

Two months after ski patrol tobogganed me off the mountain, I had surgery and began an intensive physical therapy (PT) process to rebuild strength. Three times a week I'd go to PT, where a therapist used a fancy torture device to stretch my knee before guiding me through the slowest Pilates class known to man. My doctors pushed me to work hard, but they also constantly stressed the importance of form, telling me that if we aren't attentive to form, we can develop *coping movements* that, instead of healing an injury, rely too heavily on adjacent muscle groups. Without intending it, we develop new ways of moving that, though effective and helpful in the short term, hinder our healing and open us to the possibility of new injury.

Our bodies are amazing at adapting and adopting coping movements and behaviors in the wake of an injury or trauma. Those behaviors protect us and help us survive in the wake of the fall. But if leaned on too long they begin to hinder healing, and even open us up to the possibility of new and greater injury. In the same way, our hearts are well skilled at adapting to pain and learning how to survive. Like our bodies, those skills develop quickly and often unconsciously. Sometimes we're aware of them, but often we're leaning on adjacent muscles without even realizing it. We think everything is working in harmony until we're challenged to put weight on the wound.

I think this is much closer to Jesus' understanding of sin. Sin is a learned behavior we have developed in the wake of a fall, our own or others. We've adopted skills to survive, and in many instances they have helped us do just that, but at a cost. We've leaned on muscles that are buckling under the pressure. Instead of opening ourselves up to love, we have isolated. Isolation protects us, in a way, but at a cost of the thing we need. Instead of trusting our friends we become self-reliant, protecting ourselves from another wound but at a cost of carrying too much weight on our own. Instead of wrestling with the truth of our belovedness and dignity, we work hard to build an identity we can hide behind at the cost of never being truly seen.

Original sin is all about guilt and "badness" but here I'm trying to shift our understanding of sin to one of harm and wholeness. Sin is what harms us and others and hinders our experience of wholeness. I'm not alone in this understanding—the historic church has long talked about sin in this way. A few years before Augustine of Hippo popularized *original sin*, another church father named St. Irenaeus argued that sin stems from the "old wound." Irenaeus saw in the Genesis 3 story a tale about all of humanity and the ways in which we are vulnerable to lies. We enter the world like children, beautiful and capable, but also naïve. We are susceptible, not destined, to sin because, like children raised in a disorienting environment, we can become disoriented. We can be wounded, we can hear and buy a lie, we can be led astray.

WHO IS RESPONSIBLE?

Sometimes when I use the language of wounds, harm, and trauma to describe sin, I'm accused of diminishing our responsibility for sin. That is an important objection and one worth taking seriously. We do have a responsibility, and I don't think it helps anyone to deny our agency, especially when it comes to sin. So here's how I want to respond to that objection.

First, understanding sin through the frameworks of wound, harm, or trauma does not diminish the reality, pain, or seriousness of sin. Instead, understanding sin as a painful reality connected to painful realities helps us understand why sin matters, why the writers of the Bible talk about it, and most importantly why Jesus deals with it. Sin as moral infraction is too weak of an understanding. It does not adequately express the severity of sin. Sin matters because it causes us and others real harm. That's why God cares about it.

Second, sin as law-breaking is too small a category. As we explored in chapter two, the younger son's demand for his inheritance isn't illegal, but it is painful. Or to use a positive example, in the Old Testament we read a story about a group of Hebrew midwives who lied to protect children from genocide. The midwives are later celebrated for their faith, though their words technically violated the eighth commandment. In Galatians 3:24, the apostle Paul called the Law a kind of tutor, intended to help us understand what a life of godlike love looks like. But it was never meant to be the be-all and end-all.

Finally, using the framework of wound, harm, and trauma to talk about sin helps us understand what is and what isn't our responsibility. There are parts of our stories that we cannot carry the weight of. It was not my fault my father died, nor was it your fault a parent left. Both these things are painful and have the power to wound. But we must learn what in life isn't our responsibility. What I *am* responsible for is how I respond. I am responsible for how I treat myself, God, and others. I am not responsible for what I inherited, but I am responsible for how I spend that inheritance. And that's both a compassionate and empowering perspective to take. I can have compassion on myself and others when we miss the mark, recognizing that I'm working from a complicated inheritance. At the same time, I can name my responsibility and take back my own agency. We have learned painful stories, but just as we learned them, we can unlearn those stories and learn new ones.

LEARNING A NEW NAME

After my mom married my stepdad, for a long time I called him by his name, Mark. There's nothing wrong with that, and Mark never pushed me to call him anything else. He was always gentle and kind. A part of me wanted to call him Dad. But it felt weird and hard. When you lose a parent or a loved one, you feel responsible for their story and worry your decisions or actions or choices to love again would somehow change what was. I didn't want to violate the memory of my deceased father. Which is wild, because he loved me and would of course want me to be found by another father. But just because I knew that to be true didn't mean it felt easy.

So I warmed my way into it. I didn't launch right in; I started with jokes. Humor is always the way I begin something hard or good or both. Instead of calling him Dad like a normal person, I'd whine "*Daaaad*" when I needed something. Or in a flurry of theatrical superlatives, with the accompaniment of a terrible English accent, I'd address him as "Father dearest." I've never told my dad this, and it might sound strange or silly, but I think I was learning to see my father as he already saw me. I was learning to trust; I was taking small and comical risks that engendered in me courage to take more. That's faith. I kept doing this until one day I called him Padre. I don't really know why I did it or why it stuck, but it did. Maybe it's because my parents are constantly practicing their Spanish on inno-cent waiters at their favorite Mexican restaurants. Or maybe it was because my mom, in a gross and cheesy way, calls Mark *Marcisimo*. . . honestly, I hate that I just told you that but I'm not sure how backspace works.

Whatever it was, *Padre* stuck and became for a while the primary moniker for my dad. It was a safe word, an easy place, a hiding spot in the fields where I knew I'd be okay. *Padre* taught me how to call my father by his name. Until one day—I don't remember when or even how, it wasn't intentional or rational, it just happened—I was calling him Dad. *Padre* stayed around but took a back seat to the more intimate title of Dad.

Learning to belong to God and one another is kind of like that. A slow work in love.

QUESTIONS

1. In this chapter, we talked about discipleship as the work of learning the rhythms of Jesus. How does this compare with your previous understanding of discipleship?

2. Abba Moses said we practice the Christian faith to rise step by step into love. How does this idea help you think about Christian practices (prayer, worship, reading the Bible, etc.)?

3. How does the notion of *generational sin* impact your understanding of sin and spiritual growth?

4. Are there practices that help you participate in healing that you can try this week?

Prayer

God of all prodigal brothers, I want to be home with you, but sometimes, when I'm honest, I can admit that home is hard. Sometimes it's hard to sit across from my siblings. Sometimes it's hard to feel at ease. Sometimes my old habits rear their head. Sometimes the music is annoying, and I just need to step outside. I believe you want me at the table, but help me know it. Help me risk in love so that I can *know* what has always been true, that I belong with you. Help me extend the love you give to my siblings so that we can experience together our shared belonging in you.

Amen.

P.S. Can we have tacos tomorrow?

EIGHT

Prodigal People

I REALLY, REALLY, dislike airports. I love to travel and am fine with flying. But airports, that's a different story. This is a really privileged problem to have, I admit that, but I think we can all admit that airports are absurd places. It's the overpriced plastic-wrapped sandwiches, the way you hurriedly disrobe at security like an anxious high schooler, the way I can sneak a Taser past TSA but not a package of lentils. It's all the flashing numbers on overhead screens that make you feel like you know when a plane is going to arrive even though only God knows. But really, what I hate is the waiting. You wait in line to get in. You wait for a coffee. You sit and wait for your plane, where you then wait to arrive at another airport, where you wait for a ride to take you to your destination. Airports feel like purgatory if purgatory was the fever dream of an overworked prison administrator.

For me, airports provoke an anxious kind of waiting. I check the time, get there early, check the time, try my best not to get pulled from security, check the time, get pulled from airport security because I look sketchy, and then check the time again. My wife loves this game.

Sometimes I think the Christian life can feel a bit like an airport. We know Jesus is at work bringing about the restoration of all things, and we also know it's not here yet. So we wait. Maybe we buy an overpriced sandwich, pretend like we're working, or watch the flashing numbers on the screen to see if Jesus will be on time. All of it is defined by waiting for something else. Maybe the sandwich isn't too bad, and maybe you did get a little bit of work done, but really we're just waiting for the plane to arrive so that we can shut our laptops and get out of here.

There is another way to wait, though. It's less like waiting at an airport and more like waiting for a wedding. My wife and I were engaged for just over a year before we got married (thirteen months and eleven days, but who's counting). It was a full and busy year; we had a wedding to plan, invites to send, and on top of it all we needed to find a home where we could start our new lives together. For a year we did all the work we could, but then as the day approaches, you realize there is only so much left that you can do. The big things are handled, or if they're not, they're not. And now you have family and friends in town who want to help but will distract you from the remaining details. Suddenly, you're trying to balance presence and projects. There's décor to arrange, uncles to harass, and a playlist to finalize, but there are also loved ones to see, friends to hug, and moments to remember.

On the night before our wedding, Tory and I, with our wedding party, head to the old Methodist church Tory grew up in to rehearse our ceremony. Rehearsals are not the wedding, but they are still important and beautiful because they're an enactment of what is to come. We practice walking down the aisle, which is weirdly hard to get right. We take our positions at the altar; the groomsmen immediately forget where to stand and need to be rearranged by an aunt. We look towards the back, where Tory enters resplendent. She'll be beautiful tomorrow, but this moment is worth waiting in. Once together, our pastor reminds us of the order of events, which for us centered on communion. There was no bread or wine at rehearsal, so it was like practicing practicing the gospel together. Then our pastor tells us when and how he'll announce us as a married couple, a kind of prelude good news, to which we still all shout and sing, and toss back a few beers. After the rehearsal we go to a rehearsal dinner, a sort of party before the party, a table practice. And there we sit, with family and friends from across the world, some of whom I've never met but all of whom belong together in the coming celebration of love. We tell stories, do toasts, laugh loud, and spill a little wine. It's the not the party to come, but it's a pretty good preparation for it. I think waiting, as a Christian, can be a bit more like this.

THE WEDDING AT THE END OF IT ALL

The biblical story ends with a wedding. It's the ultimate prodigal party, the celebration of homecoming, restoration, and renewal. We wait for this party. But we don't wait aimlessly. We're not stuck in an airport, twiddling our thumbs until our plane arrives. Our waiting is like that of a wedding party, in which we rehearse and practice the celebration to come. There's work to do, sure, but our primary project is presence. We're here, learning to belong together in the glory of love.

Our work is to practice our belonging as witnesses to the wedding celebration to come. It's imperfect, every rehearsal is, but that's the point. We gather at tables, forgive and ask forgiveness, welcome our siblings, see each other resplendent, and in all of it enact the gospel—the restoration of all things. This is what it means to be the people of God, the church. We are invited to live the future now. To embrace God's story and imperfectly practice Jesus' party as a sign and foretaste of the party to come.

WHAT THE CHURCH

Church can be an uncomfortable word and an even more uncomfortable proposition. Many of you reading this book have had painful encounters with religious institutions and local church communities, me included. Some of my most treasured memories come from church, but it's also the place where I've gained my deepest wounds. I've been hurt and I've hurt. I've seen friends and loved ones wounded, and I grieve the way churches have failed to stand up to injustice and participated in the perpetuation of injustice.

Often, friends of mine who have left the local church will ask me why I stay. I've thought of leaving, and there are moments when people should leave churches. But here is why I stay; I believe the church can be something beautiful. I believe the people of God can witness to the party to come through our shared practice of belonging. I believe we can make the gospel real, here and now, by stubbornly refusing to give up on one another. I believe that when we imperfectly try to love one another like Jesus loves us, we do "proclaim the Lord's death until he comes" (1 Corinthians 11:26 NIV).

When I say *church* I don't necessarily mean local institutions with paid clergy like me. Local churches, like the one I participate in, can be the church, but we're not the only or even the most important way church is expressed. What I mean by *church* is both bigger and smaller than local institutional expressions. It is, first and foremost, people who follow Jesus and practice loving like Jesus together. We are a people who belong together because of Jesus and who try to extend belonging to everyone around us. This can and does happen in formal gatherings of institutional churches, but just as often church happens around dinner tables, at backyard barbecues, in neighborhood bars, and at local city council meetings. Like the gospel we practice, church happens at the most surprising of times and in the most unlikely places. To place church within the framework of the parable of the prodigal son, church is what happens when the family is reunited at the table, when we practice our belonging together as a witness to the party to come.

THE MYSTERY

Belonging is essential to the story of God. The apostle Paul goes so far as to say our shared belonging has always been the plan of God, writing,

> Earlier generations didn't know this hidden plan that God has now revealed to his holy apostles and prophets through the Spirit. This plan is that the Gentiles would be coheirs and parts of the same body, and that they would share with the Jews in the promises of God in Christ Jesus through the gospel. (Ephesians 3:5–6)

Older translations of Paul's letter use the word *mystery* instead of *plan*, which I really like. There is something mysterious about belonging together in Christ. It is mysterious that somehow you and I would find a home together when so much about our lives and lived experiences testify to division. Practicing belonging in a world that is constantly being rent apart at the seams is a protest of hope. In our sheer stubborn insistence on the belovedness of everyone, we give witness to a possible world made real in Jesus.

A figure who understood the power of "practicing belonging" was the Reverend Dr. Martin Luther King Jr. Near the end of the Montgomery bus boycott, the Montgomery Improvement Association held a weeklong training on nonviolence and social change. Reverend King addressed the crowd, saying,

> We have before us the glorious opportunity to inject a new dimension of love into the veins of our civilization. There is still a voice crying out in terms that echo across the generations, saying "Love your enemies, bless them that curse you, pray for them that despitefully use you, that you may be the children of your Father. . . in Heaven." . . . The end is reconciliation, the end is redemption; the end is the creation of the beloved community.[1]

The "beloved community" is the kind of people who give chase to the world to come. A people who refuse to let divisions and systems of injustice remain but insist on the power of love to transform all things, even us. And that is mysterious. It's a strange and wonderful kind of mystery that rarely makes sense in a world of power games and coercive manipulations. It doesn't look efficient or even all that effective, yet we know that things like money, power, and control have never been enough to bring dead things to life or lost things truly home. No, only love does that.

WITNESS

After his resurrection, Jesus spent forty days with his friends, teaching them about the party to come and telling them, "You will receive power when the Holy Spirit has come upon you, and you will be my witnesses in Jerusalem, in all Judea and Samaria, and to the end of the earth" (Acts 1:8). We haven't talked much about Spirit in this book, but we must here, because Jesus directly connects our "witness" to the power and presence of Spirit (I will often refer to the Holy Spirit as Spirit throughout this section to personalize a member of the divine community who is often talked about in impersonal ways). Part of the mystery of God's plan to make us a people is the fact that we are aided in this work by the power of God's presence with us. What does that power look like?

A few verses after he talked about God's mysterious plan, Paul prays this, which I think is helpful for understanding the power of the Spirit:

> This is why I kneel before the Father. Every ethnic group in heaven or on earth is recognized by him. I ask that he will strengthen you in your inner selves from the riches of his glory through the Spirit. . . I ask that you'll have the power to grasp love's width and length, height and depth, together with all believers. I ask that you'll know the love of Christ that is beyond knowledge so that you will be filled entirely with the fullness of God. (Ephesians 3:14–19)

Paul asks Spirit to give us the *power* to "grasp love's width and length, height and depth, together with all believers." I love this. The power of the Spirit is a gift of knowing love that is beyond knowing, with others.

But notice the second line of Paul's prayer: "Every ethnic group in heaven or on earth is recognized" by God. Without a bit of historical context, this verse may feel random to our modern sensibilities—why wouldn't God recognize every ethnic group?—but the importance of this verse becomes clear when we look at how the early church, like us, struggled with racial divisions. The Jewish people had long been oppressed by their Gentile neighbors, namely Rome, and when Romans began converting to Christianity it caused serious contention. So much so that the church had to host multiple conventions and Paul had to write multiple letters to try and address the racism that was coming out in the church, and even then Paul had to confront the apostle Peter in Galatians for racially segregating when the church practiced Jesus' meal together (Galatians 2).

Racism sets the context for Paul's prayer. He is praying that the church would be empowered by the Spirit to overcome systemic and cultural barriers to belonging. That the church would be so confronted by love that they could not help but fight for the shared belonging of their brothers and sisters. This is the power of Spirit, and it's a power we see in vivid display when Spirit first arrives to the church.

PENTECOST

The very first miracle of Spirit comes in Acts 2, which is often understood to be the birth of the church. The disciples are gathered in Jerusalem, waiting as Jesus told them to for the Spirit to arrive, when suddenly, "All of them were filled with the Holy Spirit and began to speak in other languages, as the Spirit gave them ability" (Acts 2:4 NRSVue).

Can you imagine how disorienting this would be for the disciples? Randomly speaking a foreign language would be weird enough as it is, but the disciples have long hoped God's work would continue to center on Israel—hearing the languages of their oppressors was not what they expected of the long-awaited Spirit. That's why the early church struggled with the inclusion of Gentiles. Spirit is disrupting an exclusive party with too few chairs by redesigning the table altogether. One moment you're asking God to make Israel powerful enough to defeat Rome, in the next you're speaking Latin. The disciples receive power but not as they imagined. This is the power of reconciliation, of participation, and of a new kind of party. A party bigger and better than we imagined, one that doesn't operate like the parties of the world, but one that looks and acts like Jesus.

Spirit is here to disrupt us, empower us, and instill within us the knowledge of love so that we can practice belonging together. Spirit is like the members of a wedding party who have arrived to help us prepare for the party. Yes, Spirit will help us get some of the details ironed out, but really our project is presence. We are to be present to the presence of God in and around us.

JONNY AND JUNE

I've got to confess to you at this point, that I feel like I'm out of my depth when I talk about Spirit. All this language about mystery and inner knowledge makes my head spin. Jesus feels concrete while Spirit feels ethereal, but every once in a while, Spirit does something that helps me understand in more tangible and concrete ways.

A few years ago, I was in a dark headspace. The church I served, Missio, was in the midst of heated theological debate and one of our elders was advocating that my co-pastor and I should be terminated. It was one of those times where every decision felt heavy and every situation a lose-lose. At the same time, our church property had become a refuge for house-less folks in our city. Every day, I would arrive to the building and see more tents set up on the grass and more people sleeping under our awnings. We wanted the property to be as much of a sanctuary as possible, but we were also beginning to receive criticism and even threats from our neighbors and tenants. Some of it was unfair and unjust, but every day I'd clean up feces, needles, foils, or other drug paraphernalia that had been left in the parking lot or on the lawn.

These two complicating realties continued for months. I'd show up at the building and clean up our property, then head into a meeting that sucked. But during that time, I also met a couple we'll call Jonny and June. They slept in front of our office door, which is covered by an awning above and decent foliage on each side. To get into the building, I would have to wake them up and ask them to clean up a bit so that I could pass by. We'd do this little dance every morning and, as happens in the recurring rhythms of life, we began to chat. I learned a bit about their lives, their struggle to find housing, and the barriers to employment when you don't have housing. In an odd kind of way, we became like neighbors. I'd take them coffee and they'd walk the parking lot and clean up with me. During one of our morning routines, they asked me if I'd write a letter to the housing committee on their behalf, which I did. I didn't think much about the letter until one day Jonny and June weren't under the awning in front of our offices.

The day Jonny and June were gone had already been a particularly trying one. I'd just left a six a.m. meeting with our board and was exhausted. When I arrived at the building, I felt annoyed. I didn't want to clean up feces, or drugs, or needles.

I didn't want to hear from another angry neighbor that they planned to sue us for a creating a "public nuisance." Even realizing Jonny and June were gone made me mad. I felt betrayed. Like my neighbors had just left without a word. No gratitude, no thank yous for the coffees or the letter or the endless gentle wake-ups. Nothing. I can be a real jerk.

When I opened the office door, I noticed a little white envelope on the ground that had been slid through our mail slot. There was nothing written on the envelope and it was unsealed, which made a me a little nervous. I gingerly opened the envelope and found a note and a five-dollar bill. The note said simply,

"Thanks for giving us a place to belong. We found a home. Jonny and June."

I cried.

In a rush like wind, my annoyance, impatience, frustration, and anger gave way to the startling power of grace. I did not deserve that gift and I was not prepared for it. Everywhere I looked I had seen darkness, but in the strange mystery of love, Spirit burst forth in light. Maybe this moment seems small and insignificant to you but after I collected myself, I told my co-pastor what happened, and she cried a bit with me because of how strange and good this gift was. There was just something so surprising and confrontational about this small mercy. It upended my suspicion and reminded me of the truth of our shared belonging. That little envelope carried good news.

I think this is often how Spirit works. In the dark and dead places of life, Spirit brings light and life. Spirit whispers words of love and welcome and sometimes confronts us with reminders of our shared belonging. Spirit, through Jonny and June, did just that. In my annoyance I'd drawn the circle of belonging close to me. My party was a table of one and I'd whine at it if I wanted. But then Spirit arrived with party guests who enlivened the whole affair in the resplendent glory of love.

I wonder if my encounter with Jonny and June was at all like Pentecost. One moment, the disciples were hiding, praying, and waiting, but then in a rush they're confronted with something so good that they run into the streets to spread the news to people who, just some forty days before, had killed Jesus. Spirit arrived and expanded the disciples' circle of belonging, first in Jerusalem but then to the ends of the earth.

A LITTLE BREAD AND WINE

How do we experience the power of Spirit? This might sound a little circular, but stay with me—we practice our belonging together. Spirit is already on the move, working ahead of us, beyond us, behind us, all around us. Our job is to pay attention and join the Spirit's work. To say this even more simply, we do what Jesus did and let Spirit take care of the rest.

I think the best way to begin is at a table with a meal. Jesus loved to party, so be like Jesus and throw a party. It doesn't have to be elaborate, some of my favorite parties have been as simple as a few people eating pizza out of a box, drinking wine out of a box, sitting at a picnic table that came from a box in my backyard. That's bread, wine, and a table—what else do you need?

Start with a meal and then learn to ask curious questions. Curious questions are the kind that do not assume an answer or have a premeditated angle. A good curious question is open-ended and creates space for genuine reflection and answer, but just as important as the question itself is the posture the asker takes. The goal is knowing and being known, not leading a conversation to a specific end. Curious questions are the opposite of the survey I talked about in chapter 1, which was a tool to control the direction of a conversation. Curious questions and question-askers are here for the story, wherever it goes. When we're curious, we want to know a person, not in a voyeuristic way but in a relational and mutual kind of way. But here's the risk—if you ask curious questions then you need to be willing to answer them, too. You don't have to share all of it at first, and in fact, if you're a person prone to oversharing it can be helpful to moderate so that you leave space for everyone else. Try a little vulnerability; tell your story. Talk about faith and life, how you're trying to follow Jesus but it's not always easy. Let people in a little and with time and space, let them in a little more.

Here's the real hard part. Do it again and then again. Keep sharing meals with one another until acquaintances become friends and friends become family. Listen to one another, until the answers to questions become reasons to ask another, or to celebrate, or to mourn, or even to stop asking and just sit with each other. Practice vulnerability until it becomes confession, forgiveness, confrontation, repair, and reconciliation. The practice is in the repetition, the belonging in the rhythm.

This may all sound overly simplistic. It is. That doesn't mean it's easy, but it is simple. I have found the simplicity of practicing our belonging together can belie its significance. Sometimes eating boxed pizza with boxed wine feels holy and other times it doesn't. Sometimes a meal, a party, or a confession goes exactly as you hoped. Sometimes it doesn't. This is where we must learn to trust Spirit.

In certain Christian traditions, the celebration of Jesus' table is preceded by an ancient prayer called the *epiclesis*. Epiclesis means "invocation" and is a way of both inviting Spirit and attuning ourselves to Spirit's present activity. The prayer is simple, each version of it focusing on Spirit's activity at the table. The prayer goes something like this:

> *Spirit, make these gifts of bread and wine*
> *the body and blood of Jesus*
> *that we may be for the world the body and blood of Jesus.*
> *Make us one with Jesus and with each other,*
> *and bring us, with all creation, into your kingdom.*

It's a prayer that God would meet us at the table and transform a simple meal into something more. The elements don't change, it's still bread and juice or boxed pizza and boxed wine. What changes is us, our participation and awareness of the Spirit's work to make us one with Jesus and with each other as a witness to the world.

I've begun to offer this prayer before nearly every interaction with other people. Most of the time I'm just quietly praying it to myself before the door opens and guests arrive. Other times, I'm praying it under my breath when I run into a particularly difficult person at the store. I'm asking Spirit to meet me in the ordinary rhythm of human life. To help me pay attention and see beauty bursting forth all around me. To take my boxed pizza and boxed wine and do what only Spirit can do, transform us into the body of Jesus for the world.

PURPLE CARPETS

I grew up in a little church in Midvale, Utah, located in a shopping mall between a Family Dollar and a discount cigarette store. The building itself always had the feel of a vacated grocery store with the notable exception of purple carpets and purple chairs—which, as far as I understood, were chosen for their association with royalty. The faithful who occupied the purple thrones on a given Sunday were a ragtag crew of truckers, mechanics, ranchers, cruise ship entertainers, insurance salesmen, doctors, teachers, stay-at-home moms, and perpetually unemployed dads. Each Sunday, people donned their best, big hats and all, to drink Folgers coffee, sing along with worship CDs, listen to an hour-long sermon replete with twang and southern clichés, graciously shake hands, and then finish the afternoon with the most sacred of meals at Cracker Barrel.

After my father died, that little church became my family. The pastor was my godfather and he taught me to drive, talked to me about girls, and even let me preach from the "big stage" when I started feeling a call to pastoral ministry. Other men in the church stepped into my life to do science projects, take me camping, and help me get all my major injuries. There was an elderly woman in the church named Reba who became to me Grandma Reba, and was in every way my grandmother until she died. This little church with purple carpet loved me as best they knew how. They gave me a place to belong, to grow, and even to heal.

As life goes, I grew up, went to college, got married, and got a job at a different church. Nearly fifteen years had passed since I'd worshiped with this community or even seen many of them until, a few years ago, I got word of a funeral for a member of the community. I knew, deep inside, that I needed to attend, but honestly, I didn't want to. I felt ashamed. I hadn't seen these people in fifteen years, and I hadn't tried to stay connected. I didn't want to show up and field all the questions, explain where I'd been, or try to justify why I'd never called with empty platitudes about time. Maybe that's selfish, but family reunions are awkward when you've been gone as long as I had been.

I showed up as late as I could without missing the funeral. What a prodigal move. However, I'd forgotten the cardinal rule—God's people are never late, they arrive precisely when the party starts. I don't know what it is about Christians, but we cannot start on time—Christian Standard Time is always fifteen minutes behind—and so despite my best efforts, I arrived early. I walked into the foyer of the funeral home, hoping to grab a snack and sneak into the back of the ceremony, but as I entered the building I found, as if waiting for me, my little church. Everyone turned towards me. I recognized each one of them, and they me. It had been fifteen years, and much had changed, but not enough to disguise me. There were new lines on our faces, new wrinkles at the corner of our eyes and at the peak of our smiles. We walked a little differently, me a little taller, them a little bent. But when they saw me, they all stood tall with their faces crinkled in the direction of love. I'd hoped to hide and instead found myself the end of a good ol'-fashioned receiving line. People lined up, as is the Christian tradition, to see me. I'll never forget it. When each person approached, they did the same thing. They hugged me, took a step back to look me up and down, held me by the hand or the shoulders, and said, through smiles and tears, "Look how you've grown. . . we are so proud of you." Then as the service began, I was led to the "family seating," right behind the biological family, to sit where I belong like I'd never been gone.

I had wanted to sneak in and out, hide in the back, and go unseen and unnoticed. But my little church wouldn't let me. I belong to them and them to me, we to each other. When I was little, this church had given me a place to call home. And now they did it again. They didn't shame me for my absence, they celebrated my return. Even though I had arrived to a sad place, good news found me, confronted me, and offered me a seat at the table.

This is how we witness to belonging and the prodigal party to come. We create homes for heartsick kids and anxious older brothers. We celebrate returns and wonder at growth. We do for one another what God does for us. Our witness is our belonging; it is the revelation of the great mystery in Christ that I could somehow be at home with you. We practice our belonging until our imaginations are so saturated with welcome that we cannot help but move outwards until no person is outside the circle of belonging. We chase our siblings into the fields, we wait for them on the roads, we join those who have been left out or abandoned, we refuse to give up on people until they stop giving up on themselves, and then we refuse some more. We take the prodigal party to every forgotten corner of our world so that everyone who has been forgotten will know, "We're so glad you're home."

QUESTIONS

1. Do you have a people to practice belonging with? If not, are there steps you can take to find or form a community of belonging?

2. Are there things that make belonging particularly difficult for you to practice? What is a risk you can take or a skill you can develop to aid you in your practice?

3. The Spirit can be disruptive and challenging. Are there any places in your life that you feel the Spirit challenging and pressing on?

Prayer

Spirit, meet us in our everyday rhythms and make us aware of your disruptive love. Please transform our simple practice of meeting together at lunch tables, church alters, dinner tables, backyard barbecues, and local bars into expressions of the body and work of Jesus. You are ahead of us, behind us, all around us, but sometimes you're hard to see. So help us see, pay attention, and participate in the work you're doing so that we, with you, might witness to the wedding at the end of it all.

Amen.

A Final Word

WE HAVE COVERED a lot of ground in this book. What began with the parable of the prodigal son became an exploration of massive ideas like atonement, Trinity, Spirit, church, sin, redemption, and more often than I expected, my own life. To talk about the gospel, we had to talk about a lot of other things too.

On one hand, the gospel is a simple thing. It is the good news story of Jesus—his whole story that reveals the whole love of God. If that's all you got from this book, it would be enough. And yet, at the same time, the gospel is a story that crisscrosses the universe, time, history, and space itself. It's the story of what God is up to, what God has always been up to, and the story God is inviting us to participate in, here and now.

The gospel is Jesus' story, but it is also our story. Throughout this book I told you *a lot* about myself; I'm sorry about that. When I set out to write *Prodigal Gospel*, I didn't intend for it to include so much of me. But on reflection, how could it not? The gospel is not a set of abstract ideas to study from a safe distance; it is a living reality, beckoning each and every one of us into a life-altering encounter with Jesus. My story runs throughout this book about the gospel because our stories are a part of the gospel story.

I tell you this for two reasons. First, because your story is also a part of the good news story Jesus is writing. I don't know who you are, where you come from, or what you've experienced, but I genuinely believe the gospel includes you. The gospel is for you and me and every sibling in between. Maybe the story you inherited was heavy and backbreaking. Maybe it was terrifying and shame-inducing. Maybe this is the first time you've heard the gospel. My prayer is that as you come to the end of this book, you would feel a new or renewed desire to take a risk towards Jesus. I've provided prayers and questions to help you in this regard, but I understand that it might still feel uneasy or uncertain. I think the best next step is to find a friend who can partner with you. That can be as simple as someone who will listen or even someone who will share a weekly meal with you as you practice belonging together. I'm also going to do something a little unorthodox and put my email here (jonnydmorrison@ gmail.com). I'd be delighted to talk with you, to hear your story, and to serve as a resource or a guide, if I can.

Secondly, I hope you'll tell your story. The gospel is your story to tell, and few things are more powerful than a real story, told by real people, about their real lives. Real stories can be hard to tell, and they often take a kind of compassionate patience to tell in fullness. Sometimes we have to reckon, reconcile, heal, and even confront parts of our stories before we know how to tell them. This is hard but good work that enables us to tell a powerful, liberating, and provocative gospel to ourselves and those around us. Your story is worth telling.

Finally, if you're like me, you probably have a lot of unanswered questions. That's great! I never intended this book to be the end of your journey, my prayer is simply that it could be a help. Like a signpost on the road or a water station on the marathon run of life and faith. Keep digging, constructing, deconstructing, reconstructing, raveling, unraveling, and reforming. One of my favorite New Testament stories comes after the resurrection of Jesus. The disciple Thomas hears that Jesus is alive, but because that's a wild thing to believe, he doubts. Jesus then appears to Thomas and invites him to investigate and question (John 20:24–29). Jesus offers Thomas his very self and says, "Ask away friend." Jesus says the same to us, "Ask away friend"—the gospel is good enough to endure a little tire-kicking.

So keep asking, keeping telling your story, and take some risks. All in all, that sounds like the making of a pretty good party to me. I'll wait for an invite.

Your little brother,
Jonny Morrison

Acknowledgments

Writing a book is a real team project. Without the help of so many, this book would never have seen the light of day. I first want to thank the entire team at Herald Press, who were a joy to partner with. They believed in the idea before the idea existed and provided such helpful feedback and support along the way. Second, I want to thank everyone who read this book in its early stages, especially Keri, who edited and reviewed the earliest iterations with kindness and thoughtfulness. Third, I want to thank Missio Dei, the church I call home. The people of Missio gave me space to write, but more importantly, a place to practice belonging. You've let me lead and stumble with grace. You've watched me grow up, with all the weirdness it brings, consistently meeting me with love.

Next I want to thank my co-pastor Heather, who has been the absolute best co-worker and dialogue partner a guy could ask for. Thank for you taking on additional responsibilities as I wrote. Thank you for reading early chapters and giving both feedback and the kind of encouragement that helped me believe this thing was worth doing. And thanks for sharing a vision of the love of Jesus that feels worth working towards. I want to thank my friends who have put up with all my constant questions, who have taught me the beauty of table, and who so beautifully practice belonging.

I want to thank my parents—Jane Ann, Mark, and David—who showed me what love is. Your example was and is a living embodiment of the gospel. Finally, I want to thank my wife, Tory. Everything in this book is but a footnote to what I learn from you about love and belonging every day. You create spaces of beauty, goodness, and love everywhere you go. Thank you for journeying with me, for enduring long nights and anxious mornings as I worked. Thanks for asking me if my book was done every single day for six months. Thank you for being my friend.

Notes

Epigraph

1 Robert Farrar Capon, *Kingdom, Grace, Judgment: Paradox, Outrage, and Vindication in the Parables of Jesus*, combined ed. (Grand Rapids, MI: Eerdmans, 2002), 293.

Introduction

1 Almeda M. Wright, *The Spiritual Lives of Young African Americans*, (New York: Oxford University Press, 2017), 3,

2 Bradley Jersak, *A More Christlike God: A More Beautiful Gospel* (Pasadena, CA: Plain Truth Ministries, 2016).

Chapter 1

1 Scot McKnight, *The King Jesus Gospel: The Original Good News Revisited*, rev. ed. (Grand Rapids, MI: Zondervan, 2016), 98.

2 McKnight, 96.

3 McKnight, 98.

4 J. W. Buck, *Everyday Activism* (Grand Rapids, MI: Baker Books, 2022), 50.

Chapter 2

1 Kenneth E. Bailey, *Finding the Lost Cultural Keys to Luke 15* (St. Louis: Concordia Publishing, 1992), 116.

2 Bradley Jersak, *A More Christlike God: A More Beautiful Gospel* (Pasadena, CA: Plain Truth Ministries, 2016), 198.

Chapter 3

1 Brené Brown, *Daring Greatly: How the Courage to Be Vulnerable Transforms the Way We Live, Love, Parent, and Lead*, reprint ed. (New York: Avery, 2015).

2 Slavoj Zizek, *Violence: Six Sideways Reflections*, 1st ed. (New York: Picador, 2008), 89. cultural critic and agent provocateur Slavoj Žižek constructs a fascinating new framework to look at the forces of violence in our world. Using history, philosophy, books, movies, Lacanian psychiatry, and jokes, Slavoj Žižek examines the ways we perceive and misperceive violence. Drawing from his unique cultural vision, Žižek brings new light to the Paris riots of 2005; he questions the permissiveness of violence in philanthropy; in daring terms, he reflects on the powerful image and determination of contemporary terrorists.

3 James Baldwin, *The Fire Next Time*, reissue ed. (New York: Vintage, 1992), 10. *The Fire Next Time* galvanized the nation and gave passionate voice to the emerging civil rights movement. At once a powerful evocation of James Baldwin's early life in Harlem and a disturbing examination of the consequences of racial injustice, the book is an intensely personal and provocative document. It consists of two "letters," written on the occasion of the centennial of the Emancipation Proclamation, that exhort Americans, both black and white, to attack the terrible legacy of racism. Described by The New York Times Book Review as "sermon, ultimatum, confession, deposition, testament, and chronicle. . . all presented in searing, brilliant prose," *The Fire Next Time* stands as a classic of our literature.

4 Robert Farrar Capon, *Kingdom, Grace, Judgment: Paradox, Outrage, and Vindication in the Parables of Jesus*, combined ed. (Grand Rapids, MI: Eerdmans, 2002), 301.

Chapter 4

1 Colin E. Gunton, *Father, Son and Holy Spirit: Toward a Fully Trinitarian Theology*, 1st ed. (London, New York: T & T Clark International, 2003), 180–81.

2 Jürgen Moltmann, *The Trinity and the Kingdom: The Doctrine of God* (Minneapolis: Fortress Press, 1981), 174.

3 Robert Farrar Capon, *Kingdom, Grace, Judgment: Paradox, Outrage, and Vindication in the Parables of Jesus*, combined ed. (Grand Rapids, MI: Eerdmans, 2002), 294.

4 Scot McKnight, *A Community Called Atonement: Living Theology* (Nashville, TN: Abingdon Press, 2010), xiii.

5 Brian Zahnd, *A Farewell to Mars: An Evangelical Pastor's Journey Toward the Biblical Gospel of Peace* (Colorado Springs, CO: David C. Cook, 2014), chap. 4.

6 Bradley Jersak, *A More Christlike God: A More Beautiful Gospel* (Pasadena, CA: Plain Truth Ministries, 2016), 243.

7 A. W. Tozer, *The Knowledge of the Holy* (Fig, 2017), 1.

Chapter 5

1 Bradley Jersak, *A More Christlike God: A More Beautiful Gospel* (Pasadena, CA: Plain Truth Ministries, 2016), 270.

2 Scot McKnight, *A Community Called Atonement: Living Theology* (Nashville, TN: Abingdon Press, 2010), 23.

Chapter 6

1 N. T. Wright, ed., *Jesus and the Victory of God*, 5th ed. (Minneapolis: Fortress Press, 1997), 130.

2 Brennan Manning, *The Ragamuffin Gospel: Good News for the Bedraggled, Beat-Up, and Burnt Out* (Colorado Springs, CO: Multnomah, 2005), 61.

3 Henri J. M. Nouwen, *The Return of the Prodigal Son: A Story of Homecoming*, illust. ed. (New York: Image, 1994), 123.

Chapter 7

1 John Cassian, *The Conferences*, trans. Boniface Ramsey, annotated ed. (New York: Paulist Press, 1997), 41.

2 Kosuke Koyama, *Three Mile an Hour God*, new ed. (London: SCM Press, 2021), 7.

3 Henri J. M. Nouwen, *The Return of the Prodigal Son: A Story of Homecoming*, illust. ed. (New York: Image, 1994), 46–47.

4 Douglas A. Campbell, *Pauline Dogmatics: The Triumph of God's Love* (Grand Rapids, MI: Eerdmans, 2020), 129. Douglas Campbell offers a distinctive overview of the apostle's thinking that builds on Albert Schweitzer's classic emphasis on the importance for Paul of the resurrection. But Campbell—learning here from Karl Barth—traces through the implications of Christ for Paul's thinking about every other theological topic, from revelation and the resurrection through the nature of the church and mission. As he does so, the conversation broadens to include Stanley Hauerwas in relation to Christian formation, and thinkers like Willie Jennings to engage post-colonial concerns. But the result of this extensive conversation is a work that, in addition to providing a description of Paul's theology, also equips readers with what amounts to a Pauline manual for church planting. Good Pauline theology is good practical theology, ecclesiology, and missiology, which is to say, Paul's theology belongs to the church and, properly understood, causes the church to flourish. In these conversations Campbell pushes through interdisciplinary boundaries to explicate different aspects of Pauline community with notions like network theory and restorative justice. The book concludes by moving to applications of Paul in the modern period to painful questions concerning gender, sexual activity, and Jewish inclusion, offering Pauline navigations that are orthodox, inclusive, and highly constructive. Beginning with the God revealed in Jesus, and in a sense with ourselves, Campbell progresses through Pauline ethics and eschatology, concluding that the challenge for the church is not only to learn about Paul but to follow Jesus as he did.

5 Bradley Jersak, "'Sin'? Missing What Mark?," Christianity Without the Religion/Plain Truth Ministries, August 17, 2023, https://www.ptm.org/sin-missing-what-mark-brad-jersak.

6 "At the Cross by Isaac Watts," Great Christian Hymns, accessed November 13, 2023, https://www.greatchristianhymns.com/at-the-cross.html.

7 Charles Haddon Spurgeon, *C. H. Spurgeon's Autobiography: The Life of the Great Baptist Preacher - Compiled from His Diary, Letters, Records and Sermons* (Scotts Valley, CA: CreateSpace Independent Publishing Platform, 2017), 112, 93.

8 J. D. Greear, "3 Reasons God's Holiness Terrifies Us," JD Greear Ministries, September 7, 2015, https://jdgreear. com/3-reasons-gods-holiness-terrifies-us/.

9 John Piper, "I Know God Loves Me, but Does He Like Me?," Desiring God, accessed November 13, 2023, https://www .desiringgod.org/interviews/i-know-god-loves-me-but-does-he -like-me.

10 Krispin Mayfield and K. J. Ramsey, *Attached to God: A Practical Guide to Deeper Spiritual Experience* (Grand Rapids, MI: Zonder- van, 2022), 87–109.

11 Bessel A. Van der Kolk, *The Body Keeps the Score: Brain, Mind, and Body in the Healing of Trauma* (Penguin Publishing Group, 2015), 21.

Chapter 8

1 "(1955) Martin Luther King Jr., 'The Montgomery Bus Boycott'," BlackPast, January 17, 2012, https://www.blackpast.org/african -american-history/1955-martin-luther-king-jr-montgomery -bus-boycott/.

The Author

JONNY MORRISON is co–lead pastor at Missio Dei in Salt Lake City, Utah, responsible for teaching and vision. He's passionate about helping people gain a bigger imagination for God, experience the radical love of Jesus, and learn to see and join God's work in their everyday lives. Jonny has a master's degree in exegetical studies from Western Seminary and a doctorate in contextual theology from Northern Seminary. He writes regularly for the website Missio Alliance and the Jesus Collective, where he is on the extended leadership team.

Jesus Collective

About Jesus Collective

God is at work raising up a movement of churches, ministries, and disciples all around the world that are passionate about advancing a Jesus-centered, Jesus-looking kingdom.

This is a movement with roots in the Radical Reformation that welcomes Jesus followers from a wide range of backgrounds, traditions, and contexts. We place Jesus at the center of everything, choosing in our differences to unite around Christ in our increasingly post-Christian and polarized world.

Jesus Collective exists to amplify this movement, providing resources and relationship for those who choose to participate in more hopeful Jesus-centered expressions of faith.

In partnership with Herald Press, we are pleased to offer a line of books to fuel the Jesus-centered movement and provide vision for a more hopeful and relevant vision of Jesus in this cultural moment.

Learn more at JesusCollective.com.